INTRODUCTION

WHO ARE WEEKEND GARDENERS?

Most weekend gardeners are busy people who nevertheless want time in their lives for the feel of cool earth, for the solace of planting, for the joy of bloom, for the satisfaction of growing, and for the taste of fresh- picked produce. They want the most from their flower and vegetable gardens, but also want to achieve this goal using the least amount of time and effort.

This book offers time-saving tips and routines that will enable you to spend less time performing tedious chores and more time getting down to the business of gardening. With these tips in hand, both novice and experienced gardeners will be able to visualize the design, installation, and maintenance of their gardens before they actually begin digging.

Having a garden, appreciating its beauty, and reaping its bounty is extremely rewarding, and it allows everyone — even the person with limited time — to feel the pride that comes from creating something worthwhile. So dig in and enjoy yourself!

Chapter 1

Getting Organized...Getting Started

The secret to being a good weekend gardener is being well prepared and organized. If you tend a garden for the joy of it, you don't want to be a slave to it. The successful weekend gardeners are those who have planned effectively: the layout of the garden, the choice of plants, and a schedule of seasonal jobs and regular maintenance that, timed properly, saves later grief. Five minutes spent now can save an hour in the future.

To get started, you should decide what you want from your land. Whether you've lived with your landscape for years, have inherited a garden from previous owners, or are planning a new plot, take time to weigh your choices. Make sure your garden is more paradise than punishment.

You must face up to the need for maintenance of your entire yard and make changes that will simplify all your gardening chores. As you think about those chores, you should ask yourself a number of questions: How much time do I want to spend working the land? Would I prefer devoting my limited time to growing only fruits and vegetables or flowers? How large a garden do I want? Have my needs changed over the years, and have I had the courage to change the garden to reflect those changed needs?

Asking the Experts

In seeking answers to these questions, ask the experts and avoid making costly or time-consuming mistakes. Consult your county's Agricultural Extension Agent, a rich source of general gardening information, literature, and guidance. (Look in the phone book under the county government listings for your own or neighboring counties.) He or she can give you tips on what varieties of trees, shrubs, flowers, and vegetables grow well in your climate and soil type. He or she can also test your soil and tell you if it's alkaline or acid — a critical question that will directly impact your ability to grow things well. Call your County Forester for information on recommended trees or advice on maintaining or improving those you already have. The Soil Conservation Service representative for your area can tell you about local soils. (Look in the phone book under U.S. government listings.) A soil survey can be helpful in making

7

decisions about land use. Some government personnel will even visit your land on request.

Basic Tools You'll Need

If you're just starting out, investing in a set of quality hand tools is a must. Nothing is more annoying than not having the right equipment for the tasks at hand. Whenever possible, select tools and implements for their comfort of use. If you're tall, you'll find that long-handled tools will save your back. Consider the weight of tools as well; there's no need to suffer shoulder ache after doing just a little cultivating or digging. The following list of essential tools will get you going:

■ **Shovel or spade** — an essential all-purpose garden tool for digging, spreading, sod-slicing, and stone-prying.

■ **Spading fork** — another multiple-use, indispensable garden tool. Its four heavy-gauge tines make it perfect for breaking sod, aerating soil, digging root crops, turning compost heaps, cleaning out dense animal manure and bedding, and many other tasks. All-purpose forks, commonly known as pitchforks, have five slender tines for moving lighter loads such as hay and leaves.

■ **Hoe** — a multi-purpose tool used primarily for weeding and cultivating between rows of plants, but heavier versions can be used to dig shallow furrows for planting or irrigation. The narrower the hoe, the better for cultivating between individual plants.

■ **Cultivator** — a tool that aerates the soil and chops weeds at the same time. When cultivating close to plants, take care not to damage roots by cultivating too deep.

■ **Garden rake** — another garden workhorse, the rake levels and smoothes out seedbeds prior to planting by snagging rocks, roots, and sticks. It's the perfect tool for mixing lime and fertilizer into the upper soil, and for spreading and removing mulches.

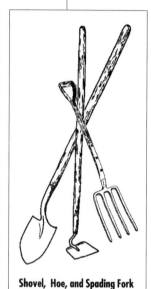

Shovel, Hoe, and Spading Fork

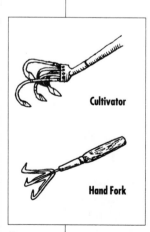

Cultivator

Hand Fork

- **Hand fork** — This helpful tool may be considered a miniature cultivator, hoe, and rake. You tend to be on all fours when using a hand fork.

- **Hand trowel** — an indispensable tool for transplanting and a handy one for applying fertilizer or compost.

- **Work gloves** — no gardener should be without them. They prevent blisters and cuts, and keep you from spending long hours cleaning your fingernails.

- **Watering equipment** — to be productive, lawns, trees, and gardens must have adequate supplies of water — particularly in areas of low rainfall. A good hose and watering can are invaluable tools.

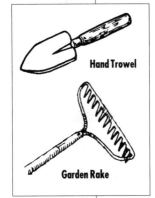

Hand Trowel

Garden Rake

WHAT ABOUT YOUR SOIL?

Rich, healthy soil is the cornerstone of all successful lawns and gardens. Good soil practically guarantees prolific yields, prevents insect and disease attack, and will make your gardens the envy of the neighborhood, not to mention making your work much easier. It promotes vigorous plant growth.

What you may not know is that building and maintaining super soil is surprisingly easy — once you know how to do it.

1. **Test your soil.** Ideally this should be done in the fall because the test labs are less busy then, and you won't have to wait as long for results. Use a hand trowel to take small amounts of soil from several spots in the garden at a depth of 6 inches. Mix the samples together in a bucket. Allow the mixture to dry at room temperature. Put a few ounces in a plastic bag, seal it, and bring it to the nearest county Agricultural Extension Service office.

    It won't be long before you get a report back indicating the basic nutrient and pH levels in your soil, along with the soil's organic content.

2. **Correct the soil pH.** The acidity or alkalinity of the soil (pH level) has a tremendous bearing on how plants and shrubs develop. A pH of 7 is neutral — below is acid, above is alkaline. Most gardens thrive in the 5.5 to 7.5 range, with

some exceptions. Your soil report will indicate the pH of your soil and how it should be adjusted.

3. **Add organic matter to the soil.** Whether your soil is predominantly clay, sand, or loam, adding organic matter (leaves, grass clippings, manure, kitchen waste, etc.) will improve the way the soil's particles cluster together. Organic matter helps to bind small particles of clay in aggregates, so that a crumbly structure is formed, with spaces for air. In a sandy soil, organic matter helps retain moisture and nutrients longer.

TO RAISE SOIL ONE UNIT OF pH

100 sq. ft.	Hydrated Lime	Dolomite	Ground Limestone
Light Soil	1½ pounds	2 pounds	2½ pounds
Heavy Soil	3½ pounds	5½ pounds	6 pounds

TO LOWER SOIL ONE UNIT OF pH

	Sulphur	Aluminum Sulphate	Iron Sulphate
Light Soil	½ pound	2½ pounds	3 pounds
Heavy Soil	2 pounds	6½ pounds	7½ pounds

Note: The amount of lime you use doesn't have to be as precisely measured as this chart suggests.

So make yourself a promise: Never plant anything — tree, shrub, plant, or seed — unless you have first replenished the soil's organic matter in some way. And how can you do that? Read on in Chapter 2.

COMPOST: THE NATURAL FERTILIZER

Successful gardeners insist that nothing can take the place of a shovelful of compost mixed in planting holes for tomatoes, peppers, eggplant, and members of the cabbage family. Melons, cucumbers, and squash need its richness to send out strong, healthy vines. Use compost to side-dress hungry crops, mix it into the seedbed, or cover fine seeds with it as you plant.

Feed your vegetables and flowers with compost, then sit back watch them grow.

What is this magic growth hormone? Compost is decomposed plant material; it looks like black, fluffy soil. Whether you make it in place as year-round mulch or in a separate bin doesn't

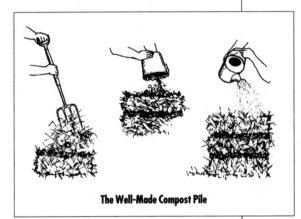

The Well-Made Compost Pile

matter. Once you've tried compost, you'll never again be able to stand looking at crusty, dried-out soil.

NO-NONSENSE COMPOSTING

If you're a purist, here's how to get a rich, fast compost.

- First, use 6 inches of green matter (weeds, leaves, grass clippings, etc.) as a base.
- Second, add 2 inches of manure, garbage, or other high-nitrogen source. Keep a half-gallon milk carton or similar container next to the kitchen sink, and get into the habit of filling it with the kitchen's vegetable and organic waste: parings, eggshells, fruit pits and rinds, coffee grounds, tea leaves, carrot tops, cabbage cores, and so on. When the carton is full, toss its contents on the compost pile.
- Third, add a sprinkling of soil (plus a little ground limestone and ground phosphate rock).

Repeat layers until the pile is 4 or 5 feet high.

Be guided by your own needs and sense of esthetics. You have to moisten each composting layer as you build the compost pile so that it is about as wet as a squeezed-out sponge. Poke holes in the pile with a rod to aid aeration. Turn the pile after 6 weeks and start using it after 3 months.

COMPOSTING MATERIALS

Materials for composting and soil enrichment need not be limited only to those you generate yourself. If you have imagination and the initiative to scavenge a bit (that time spent building your soil will mean lush crops that grow with less of your midsummer energy), here's a list of possibilities:

apple pomace (a by-product of cider-making)
bird-cage cleanings
brewery wastes
buckwheat hulls
cannery wastes
castor bean pomace
chaff
cheese whey
cocoa bean hulls
corncobs and husks
cottonseed hulls
vacuum cleaner dust
evergreen needles
feathers
felt waste
fish scraps
garden residues (spent plants and vines, beet and carrot tops, corn stalks, etc.)
grape pomace (by-product of wine making)
grass clippings
hair
hay
kitchen wastes (vegetable and fruit rinds, parings, eggshells, coffee grounds, tea leaves, etc.)
leaves
manure (horse, cow, goat, pig, rabbit, or poultry)
milk, sour
mill wastes of linen, wool, and silk
nut shells
oat hulls
peanut hulls
peat and sphagnum moss
pond weeds
rice hulls
sawdust and shredded bark
seaweed, kelp, and eelgrass
straw
sugar cane
tobacco stems
wood chips and rotted wood

For best results, your compost pile should be contained. The simplest container is a circular wire cage that you can make yourself from about 10 feet of 4-foot-high woven wire fence. If you have large quantities of material to be composted, you may want to make your circular cage larger (each 3 feet of fencing equals approximately 1 foot of diameter), or have several piles going simultaneously.

You can make compost bins from a variety of materials. A three-sided, concrete-block bin is easy to construct. Lay the blocks sideways (don't use mortar), and the holes will help let the air in and the gases out of the pile. If you want to get fancy, suspend perforated pipe at intervals between the holes in the blocks to promote even better aeration. Or lift the pile off the ground with pipes thrust between the second layer of blocks. Place wire mesh on the pipes. Evergreen branches laid on the wire will prevent most of the compost from sifting through the mesh. Build from there with composting materials. No turning is necessary, because of the 10-inch air space under the pile.

The Wire-Mesh Composting Bin

If you have limited space, you can compost in a garbage can or drum. Punch holes in the bottom and sides (for drainage and aeration), set the can on bricks or concrete blocks, and layer materials with soil inside.

Commercial compost containers are also available. Most are designed so that the finished compost can be removed through an opening near the bottom. They are quite expensive, however.

If you want to make compost fast, here are three ways to speed up the decomposition of your pile:

Concrete-Block Compost Bin

1. Increase the ratio of nitrogen to carbon in the compost pile. Materials high in carbon include wood shavings, sawdust, dry leaves, and straw. Materials high in nitrogen are fresh grass clippings, fresh manure, vegetable wastes, green vegetation, and fertilizers such as blood meal, fish meal, or alfalfa meal. Don't put too much nitrogen on your pile or you'll end up with slime.

13

2. Increase the amount of air in the pile by laying perforated pipe at intervals as you build the pile. At every foot or so in height lay a few pipes horizontally a foot or two apart.

3. Increase the surface area of ingredients by shredding them with a shredder or rotary mower before heaping them on the pile. (If you want to moisten and turn the pile after 4, 7, and 10 days' time, you can have finished compost in about two weeks.)

A Convenient Compost Pile

Whichever method you use to store your compost, where you locate the pile will influence your attitude toward it. Think of the compost pile as an easy way to dispose of waste you have to get rid of anyway. It should be near, or even in, your garden. The less hauling you have to do, the more convenient it will be to stockpile and use.

If you are a scavenger who collects composting materials from other places, try to locate your pile somewhere near your

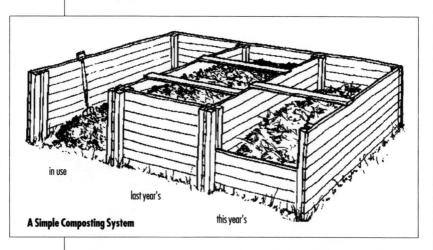

in use

last year's

this year's

A Simple Composting System

driveway as well. Finding a spot with good drainage is important; so too is the pile's proximity to a water supply, if you live in a dry climate. After all, the easiest way for a weekend gardener to ignore the compost pile is to be faced with the prospect of hooking up a hose and lugging it any great distance to water the compost. Life's too short for busy work.

Chapter 3

Choosing a Gardening Method

Many vegetable gardeners are now trying methods of planting other than the traditional method of using widely spaced rows — methods that promise larger harvests with less work. By understanding the advantages and disadvantages of each method, you will be able to determine which is best suited for your needs prior to designing your perfect plot. You can use any one of the methods described below or combine elements of two, several, or even all five.

Container/Patio Gardening

The perfect method for those people with little time, space, or desire to do extensive gardening, container gardening simply means planting vegetables or flowers in containers, whether they be redwood tubs, window boxes, strawberry pots, plastic pots, or hanging baskets.

The key is to identify the kind of container or patio garden you want. In other words, do you want a container garden of vegetables or a window box filled with scented flowers? Anything is possible, but because space is limited, don't try to do too much. Concentrate your efforts on a few containers.

A few general words of advice: Be sure to have a drainage hole in your container; be sure that your soil is nutrient-enriched and porous, to ensure that water drains properly and allows proper air circulation around the roots. It's important to know also that common backyard soil may not be good for container gardens, since it may well contain too much sand, and therefore not retain enough water; or it might contain too much clay and silt, therefore holding too much water. Because of their contained environment, you should also give your plants a dose of liquid fertilizer about once a week throughout the growing season.

The only real drawback to container gardening is that you'll have to water religiously throughout the growing season, especially on hot summer days. But the benefits of versatility — especially in being able to move plants and crops around easily — far outweigh any disadvantages.

For more specific advice on container gardening, refer to Chapter 12.

Imagine your Thanksgiving table graced with a beautiful salad of crisp baby lettuce, tangy onions, crunchy radishes, and your very own tomatoes.

While this may sound like the northern gardener's fondest fantasy, you can make it come true through the use of a simple, inexpensive cold frame. A cold frame will let you extend your growing season up to several months.

A cold frame is nothing more than a box of boards set on the ground outdoors and topped with a second-hand storm window, but its simplicity belies its usefulness. And the cost of a cold frame will be repaid many times over in plain good eating when other people have long since abandoned their gardens.

How to Build a Cold Frame

A cold frame does not have to be any specific size, but most tend to measure about 3 feet by 6 feet. Don't make the frame too wide, or you'll have trouble reaching all your plants.

INSULATED COLD FRAME

½ old storm window

styrofoam insulation

weatherstripping

2½'

16"

All you have to do is nail the ends of four fairly wide boards together to make a square or rectangle. This simple frame can then be covered with glass — an old window sash, maybe, or some sort of plastic that will let light through. It is best if this bottomless cold frame can sit on a slope that slants slightly to the south. This will provide maximum exposure to the sun's rays and will keep the box warmer.

The reason for building cold frames or hotbeds is to allow yourself time, either in the early spring or late fall, to grow plants in a place protected from frost. (Most people use cold frames more in the spring when they are starting new plants, but they can be used to extend the growing season into the fall, too.) You can either plant seeds in the ground under the box, or you can put starter flats inside it.

A cold frame will hold its own heat quite well, but it will need some extra protection on very cold nights. If you hear that the temperature is going to drop far below freezing, cover the box with a piece of canvas or an old blanket, just to be on the safe side.

Bright sun can also be something of a problem. Cheese-cloth spread over the cold frame cover will help prevent sun-burned plants.

During the day, you have to be careful not to let your cold frame overheat. On a bright, sunny afternoon, you may have to encourage air circulation by opening the window a little or by leaving the top ajar.

WIDE-ROW GARDENING

Instead of narrow rows of one plant width, wide-row gardening calls for broadcasting seed in broad bands of 10 inches or more. A row the width of a rake, about 16 inches, is most practical. This planting method allows a weekend gardener to:

- plant more quickly
- weed less — close planting leaves less space for weeds
- save water — plants form a "living mulch" that shades the earth, traps dew for added moisture, and counters drying of the soil by wind
- grow cool-weather crops for a longer period, because they won't bolt as fast
- harvest more from less space
- reap a longer harvest — since natural competitiveness of the closely spaced crop makes some plants mature earlier than others

How do you prepare a wide-row seedbed? Simple. Run string attached to two stakes the length of the garden, then line up one edge of a steel garden rake next to the string and drag it the length of the row. For a wider row, lay out two strings to the desired width and drag the rake between them.

Broadcast or sow seed in the raked area, slightly closer together than you would normally. Press the seed into the soil with the back of a hoe or rake. With the rake or hoe, pull up soil from outside the row to cover the seed. (Use enough soil to make a covering four times the seed's diameter, or, for long seeds, as deep as their length. In clay soil, you can cover a little more sparingly than in sandy soil.) Tamp down again. You can cover a planting of fine seeds with a thin layer of straw to help hold in moisture until germination.

This system works well with most vegetables, but it isn't recommended for use with potatoes, tomatoes, corn, melons, squash, or cucumbers.

RAISED-BED GARDENING

In the raised-bed system, vegetables are planted close together on beds that are built up 6 to 10 inches above ground level. Walkways run between the beds.

In the past, soil preparation for raised beds was a lot of work. It involved double-digging the soil and spading in compost, well-rotted manure, bone meal, wood ashes, and even more manure. The mere contemplation of this method would send any weekend gardener to the nearest hammock.

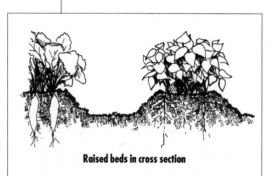

Raised beds in cross section

But there's an easier way. Start with a well-prepared seedbed, one that needn't be double-dug. Enrich it with compost, manure, other organic matter, or fertilizer. Then the raised beds can be formed using either hand tools or (even easier) a rototiller with a hilling attachment.

Proponents of raised-bed gardening claim higher yields by using this method — as much as four times more vegetables per acre than are raised by single-row gardeners. Some other advantages include the fact that:

- Drainage is improved.
- You can plant earlier, because soil warms faster and dries out more quickly in the spring.
- There's little or no weeding. Close planting leaves little room for weeds.
- The weeds that do appear are within easy reach.
- Plants provide a "living mulch," shading the soil and keeping it cooler.
- No one walks where plants are growing.
- Digging deeply in rocky or shallow soils is avoided.
- Soil, continually enriched, becomes loose and friable.

■ Beds can be formed in the fall, to be ready for an early start when wet clay soils might delay planting.

The two major disadvantages of raised beds are that:

■ Beds tend to dry out in summer heat.
■ The paths between the beds can become weedy. To overcome this problem, peel thick "leaves" from bales of spoiled hay to cover the pathways. Add more hay if weeds sprout through the first layer.

Square-Bed Gardening

In this method, the vegetable garden is laid out in square sections, 4 feet by 4 feet, with paths between the squares. As with raised beds, you always walk in the paths, never in the beds. Seed spacing is figured by the number of seeds (or transplants) per square foot. A 1-foot square of garden holds, for instance, one pepper plant or four heads of lettuce or nine beets or sixteen onions. Vining crops are trained vertically.

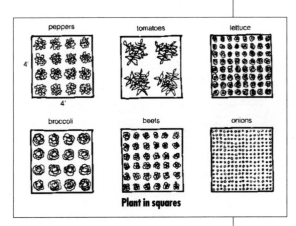

Plant in squares

Advantages of square-bed gardening include the fact that:

■ Soil is never compacted by foot traffic, because you can reach everything in the garden from the defined paths.
■ There's a greater harvest from less land — you need much less space than you would for the same harvest planted in conventional rows.
■ Less land in the garden means there's less weeding, less watering, and less compost and other materials needed to enrich the soil.
■ Overplanting is avoided.
■ The garden looks neater.
■ No thinning is needed.
■ Crop rotation is easy to figure and doesn't require elaborate planning.
■ No power tools are needed once the garden is established.

19

■ Soil is enriched bit by bit after each square foot is harvested, so no big spring soil preparation is necessary.

The only real disadvantage to square-bed gardening is that the beds take longer to plant in the spring.

Designing the Perfect Plot

Now that you know what you'd like to plant and the various methods of planting, you've got to decide where in your yard you'd like your garden. There are a few simple techniques for siting your garden that will make this an easy job.

First, note the sun's path over the course of a year. Your garden should get good morning sun and, if you're growing tomatoes, peppers, or other hot-weather crops, at least six hours' worth throughout the growing season.

Second, make sure your site is on a slight slope, so water drains properly and well.

Third, view your property from above. It will give you a new perspective as to exactly how your garden will look within the overall landscape of your yard. No, you don't have to be an artist to do this. Just get a good idea of where things will go in relation to each other. For instance, you don't want to put the garden too far from your kitchen, since that will just make harvesting more work.

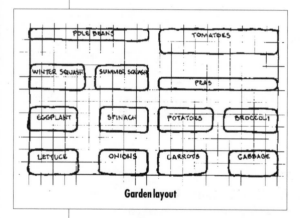

Garden layout

Once you've actually sited the garden, you must then proceed to plan the garden itself. Again, you can avoid costly and time-consuming mistakes by doing it as the pros do: Plan your garden on graph paper. Make note of each variety you're thinking of using; the height and color of each; their cultural requirements (how much water they need, how much sun, the kind of soil they like best); the spacing they need to grow best; and the companion plants that will help each.

Once you've determined what will go where, don't think your job is over. Keep a blank sheet of tracing paper with your graph and make notes: of color changes that you don't like and don't want to repeat next year; of height disparities (for instance, you might have irises planted by mistake in front of snowbells); and of other problems that you find occurring throughout the growing season. Identifying these problems before and as they occur will keep you from making the same mistakes next year — again, something that good weekend gardeners always do.

A Simple Layout

To get maximum sun, plant the tallest crops on the north side of your garden, so that they don't shade shorter ones, or make your rows run north and south.

Plant vegetable families together in order to aid in planning the rotation of crops in subsequent years.

Vegetable Families

- **Legumes:** peas, beans, limas
- **Brassicas:** cabbage, kale, broccoli, collards, cauliflower, kohlrabi, brussel sprouts
- **Cucurbits:** cucumber, melons, squash
- **Nightshades:** peppers, tomatoes, potatoes, eggplant
- **Root vegetables:** beets, carrots, turnips, salsify, parsnips, radishes, rutabagas, onions, garlic, leeks
- **Corn**
- **Leafy greens:** spinach, chard, lettuce

Maximize Your Growing Space

Take advantage of all the space you have by utilizing inter-cropping, succession planting, and vertical cropping.

- **Intercropping** means planting quick-maturing vegetables such as lettuce and spinach between widely spaced rows of a slow-maturing crop such as tomatoes, or growing squash alongside corn.
- **Succession planting** means making a second planting, such as putting in beans where you've just harvested early spinach. Make sure to dig in compost or fertilizer, though, before you replant.
- **Vertical cropping** means training sprawling plants to grow up supports. Try it with cucumbers, squash, tomatoes, melons and pole beans.

Wire cylinder

CHAPTER 4
DIGGING IN

GET A HEAD START — STARTING SEEDLINGS INDOORS

Is it really worth the trouble to start seedlings indoors, or is it more practical to wait until spring and buy the pre-grown stock you need? There are a number of good reasons to start seeds indoors. For one thing, many annuals and vegetables have such a long growing season that they won't flower or fruit if they don't get a head start indoors, especially in the North. Others may not need to be started indoors, but they will flower or be productive for a much longer time if started early. Plants with delicate seeds should be started indoors to protect them from the ravages of weather. And finally, by controlling the conditions in which plants are grown, indoor seed starting virtually eliminates worries about weeds, insects, and disease.

SOME ANNUALS THAT CAN BE STARTED INDOORS

Begonia	Petunia	Monkey Flower
Coleus	Salpiglossis	Cupflower
Geranium	Salvia	Poor-Man's Orchid
Impatiens	Browallia	Wishbone Flower
Lobelia	Ornamental Pepper	Pansy
African Marigold	Vinca	Verbena
	Gerbera	

Many vegetables can be sown directly in the garden bed, while others must be started indoors, since the growing season, in all but the warmest parts of the country, is not long enough for them to produce. These include broccoli, brussels sprouts, cabbage, cauliflower, celery, eggplant, leeks, okra, peppers, and tomatoes. Lettuce, onions, and melons are often started indoors as well, to get a jump on the growing season.

GROWING UNDER LIGHTS

If you're willing to put in the time to reap the fun of growing your own, don't fool around with narrow windowsills and straggly plants. Grow them under lights for best results.

23

You can buy a plant stand for starting seedlings — or you can invest an hour in making a stand that's fine for starting tomatoes and other plants. Here's one that's easy to build.

Materials You Will Need:

- Four 2" x 4" x 72" uprights
- Nine 2" x 2" x 48" horizontal pieces
- Four 1" x 6" x 48" sides of plant area
- One 48" x 48" particle-board or plywood shelf
- One 60" x 60" plastic sheet, for shelf covering
- Two 48" two-tube fluorescent units, with hooks and chains
- Optional: one 2" x 2" x 96" piece to be cut into four supports

PLANT STAND FOR INDOOR GROWING

48" x 48" particle board or plywood shelf

2'0" approx.

3" x 2" x 48" horizontal pieces

2" x 4" x 72" uprights

Use wood screws throughout. Construct the shelf frame and end units, then place the shelf at a height comfortable for you. Screw the two top bars into position. Mount the steel hooks into the underside of the top bars so that the light units suspended from them will be centered. Attach the shelf to the frame and add the 1" x 6" side pieces. Place the plastic sheet inside the shelf unit and fill it with peat moss. Keep the peat moss damp to increase humidity around the plants.

Buying 48-inch-long shop lights is a lot cheaper than buying fancy plant lights from a garden shop. Replace one fluorescent tube in each fixture with a Gro-light. Keep a distance of 5 to 6 inches from the top of the plant foliage to the light source, and give the plants 14 to 15 hours of light each day.

Once your stand is built, you'll want to begin planting. But don't use garden soil for indoor planting because it is likely to be loaded with pathogens. Use sterile, commercial potting mix, or make your own (see box next page).

Start your sowing process by assembling your containers and making sure they are clean and have drainage holes. If the container is made of fiber or peat, it must be soaked thoroughly before the potting soil is placed in it or it will act as a wick and pull moisture out of the growing medium later on. Fill the container with water and allow it to absorb all that it can, draining off the rest, or place the flat or pot in a larger container of water until it has absorbed all it can. When the flat is thoroughly moistened, place a layer of stones or gravel in the bottom.

To judge how many seed flats to prepare, use this rule of thumb: A 5½" x 7½" flat will hold 100 seedlings from large seeds, 200 seedlings from medium seeds, and 300 seedlings from fine seeds. Always sow about twice as many seeds as the number of plants you want, since all of the seeds won't germinate, and some seedlings will be lost in the thinning and transplanting processes.

Once your flats are ready for planting, gather together your seeds and double-check to see if they need any special treatment before sowing, such as soaking or scarification. Check the time required to germinate and grow the plants to the point where they are transplanted outdoors, so that seeding is done at the proper time.

You may not want to sow all of the seeds in each packet, just in case something goes awry and you have to start all over again. If you're sowing two types of seed in the same flat, be sure you pick ones that have the same temperature requirements and that germinate in approximately the same length of time — and make sure you write the name of the plants and the date of sowing on a label.

A good system for spacing seeds in flats is to cut a piece of 1-inch-mesh chicken wire the size of a flat. (Put it in a wooden frame, if you want to be fancy.) Lay it on top of the soil and plant

A SIMPLE POTTING MIX FORMULA

- Two parts soil
- One part compost or leaf mold
- One part sand, perlite, or vermiculite

Sterilize soil in a 150° F oven for 30 minutes, or use a microwave oven for speedy sterilization. Put the soil in a plastic bag in which you've punched a few holes. Bake it in the microwave for four or five minutes.

a seed inside each hole for 1-inch spacing. You can also plant on 2-inch or 3-inch centers.

Once your seed flats are ready, it is extremely important to place them in a location with proper light and temperature for germination — under lights is the more productive method (no worry about short and cloudy days). In the following weeks, how you care for your seedlings is critical. Water, of course, is most important. Once the second set of leaves (these are the first "true leaves") has developed, it is time to start fertilizing. No food is needed prior to this point, since the seedling is using food that was stored in the seed.

IT'S TIME TO TRANSPLANT

After the seedlings have developed four true leaves, it is time to transplant or thin them. It is possible to plant seedlings directly from the seed flat into the garden, but this is generally not advised. The seedlings should be transplanted to a larger container first, or at least thinned so they will not be crowded, leggy, weak, or susceptible to damage. One transplanting is usually enough, and will guarantee good, strong root development and easier adjustment of the plant to the garden. Seedlings that have been started in individual pots do not need to be transplanted.

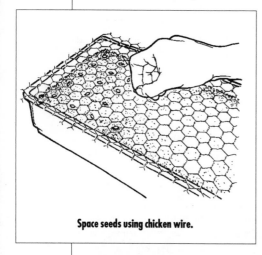

Space seeds using chicken wire.

One week before indoor-grown seedlings are shifted outdoors to the garden, begin to *harden them off*. This process acclimates the soft and tender plants, which have been protected from wind, cool temperatures, and strong sun — and gradually gets them used to their new environment.

Move the trays or flats of potted plants outside into a sheltered, shady area such as a porch, cold frame, or under a tree or shrub. If it gets cold at night, move them back inside. After two or three days, give them half a day of sun, increasing the exposure gradually to a full day. Make sure the transplants are well watered during this "hardening off" period.

After your seeds have germinated and the seedlings are growing strong and healthy, it's time to transplant them into the garden. Double-check planting dates before you start moving plants outside. Most annuals and vegetables must wait until all danger of frost is past to be placed outside, though some can go out earlier. Tomatoes, eggplant, and peppers should wait a little longer, until the ground has completely warmed up.

Your newly set-out plants may look a little sparse at first, but they will grow and fill in quickly. From this point on, a few simple maintenance practices will ensure a successful garden and a lot of enjoyment.

Chapter 5

Weeding Out

Beating the Weeds

The bane of every weekend gardener's life is trying to keep up with — and ahead of — weeds. The secret to weed control is to get them while they're still little. You must begin cultivating the weeds as soon as they appear. It's light work to knock them down then; later on, when they're firmly rooted and threatening to take over the garden, eliminating them becomes hard work. The instant that weeds appear, attack them with a hoe or rake. Do not wait for them to get a foot high, but break every inch of the surface crust of the ground just as soon as a germ of weed growth shows itself. Even better is to do this before any weeds show, for by using a small, sharp steel rake, two or three days after your crop is planted or sown, you will kill the weeds just as they are germinating.

> ## Eating the Weeds
>
> A weed really is only a plant growing where it's not wanted. Learn to love some of your weeds. Think of them as free vegetables. Don't fight them, eat them! Chopped and tossed in a salad with young scallions, dandelion greens symbolize all the vigor and strength of a new gardening year, and taste good too!

The best time to weed is after a good rain, when the soil is soft and weed roots give little resistance. Put more time into weeding in the spring and the rest of the summer you'll need to weed just one day a week. Limiting the time you spend weeding by developing a routine will help as well. Every time you take a walk through your garden, whether to collect vegetables or flowers or just to enjoy the garden's beauty, yank out the most insidious and conspicuous weeds.

Smother the Weeds with Mulch

Another easy way to keep weeds down is by using a mulch. Add to that the other virtues of mulch:

- It conserves moisture. Mulchers rarely, if ever, water crops.
- It reduces compaction of the soil when people walk on it, or when hard rain pounds it.
- It helps prevent soil erosion.
- It keeps dirt from splashing on crops during rains, so you spend less time washing leaf crops after harvest.

- It protects sprawling crops like tomatoes, melons, cucumbers, and squash against rot, since mulch prevents direct contact of fruit with the soil.
- It helps maintain an even soil temperature. Mulch helps soil stay cooler during baking-hot summer days and warmer during chilly spring and fall nights.
- It encourages earthworm activity.
- It helps improve soil fertility.

MULCHING MATERIALS

Be imaginative in collecting mulching materials. Buy if you must, or scavenge from friends or local industries. Try using some of the following materials:

- hay (a farmer might be delighted to unload spoiled bales)
- straw
- leaves (shred or rotary-mow them first)
- hulls or shells from cocoa beans, buckwheat, peanuts, rice, cottonseed, oats, or nuts
- grass clippings (ask your neighbors or a lawn-maintenance service to save them)
- wood chips (get them from a utility company pruning near overhead wires)
- shredded bark
- sawdust
- seaweed, kelp, eelgrass
- ground corncobs and stalks
- shredded sugar cane
- packing materials (excelsior, shredded paper)
- salt hay
- coffee grounds
- partially decomposed compost
- pebbles
- ground oyster shells
- newspaper
- peat moss (though it tends to cake, and is really better dug into the soil)
- Spanish moss
- tobacco stems (but keep them away from tomatoes, peppers, eggplant, and potatoes)

Note: When adding sawdust, woodchips, shredded bark, or ground corncobs or stalks to your garden as mulch, be sure to add at the same time some nitrogen-rich material like compost or manure to prevent these mulches from robbing nutrients from the soil.

A Word to the Wise

In northern climates, year-round mulch may not work as well as in moderate and southern zones. Tomatoes, for instance, are unhappy growing in cold soil. Beans need warm soil for germination, and mulch can keep the soil from warming up in early spring. Pull it back in planting areas for heat-loving crops, so that the soil can bake for a week or two before planting time. Some northern gardeners till or cultivate until the ground warms up, then mulch for the rest of the summer.

Make sure your soil is thoroughly damp before applying mulch. Otherwise, you'll be maintaining soil dryness instead of conserving soil moisture. And don't be a miser with mulch. Make it thick enough so it can do its job of surpassing weeds. Coarse mulches such as hay or straw need to be 8 to 12 inches deep. Finer mulches can be applied more thinly. Something as fine as coffee grounds needs to be spread only about ½ inch thick. When in doubt, add a little extra mulch; it will settle more quickly than you think.

It is easier to spread mulch over your entire garden, then pull it back and plant, than it is to mulch after the crops are up. If you do it the hard way, you will have the tedious work of placing mulch between and around young plants, and that takes a lot more time.

Rock Mulches

All around your landscape and flower beds, rock mulches can be used to keep down weeds and seal in moisture in the same way that other mulches are used. Rock mulches work best in large areas with few plants, or as transitional borders where pavement or some other hard surface ends and the flower beds begin. A good example is the 1-foot-wide border of rock or gravel that lines a driveway or surrounds a deck. This weed-blocking rock border can be used as a base on which to set pots, or as a buffer to keep messy mulches from spilling onto paved areas.

Dry streambeds and gravel pathways are another way to use rocks as a weed block. In areas where no plants will be grown, you can lay down black plastic and put the stone or gravel mulch on top. Poke holes in the plastic for drainage, and make sure the rock layer on top is at least 2 inches thick and completely covers the edges of the plastic undersheeting.

Volcanic rock, white rock, cinder rock, and crushed marble are all attractive rock forms that can be used for mulching.

Remember that crushed rock mulches won't improve the soil like an organic mulch, but they don't have to be replaced as often, either. Lightweight cinder rock or volcanic rock will blow around in a windstorm, and all rock mulches will collect leaves and debris over time. These are two reasons why a fresh rock layer may need to be added every two or three years to keep the pebbles looking pretty.

Full-page photo: Cabbage and ornamental plants growing in containers. JERRY HOWARD/ POSITIVE IMAGES. Inset, top: African marigolds, 'Sugar and Spice'. ANN REILLY: PHOTO/NATS. Inset, above: Japanese beetle on a flower blossom. GREG CRISCI: PHOTO/NATS.

Full-page photo: Planting tools. ANN REILLY: PHOTO/NATS. **Inset, left: Black plastic mulch.** JERRY HOWARD/POSITIVE IMAGES. **Inset, right: Straw mulch placed between garden rows.** JERRY HOWARD/POSITIVE IMAGES.

Full-page photo: Preparing screens for pea plants. DON JOHNSTON: PHOTO/NATS. **Inset, left: Making a raised bed.** JERRY HOWARD/POSITIVE IMAGES. **Inset, right: Working garden soil with a rototiller.** DON JOHNSTON: PHOTO/NATS.

Full-page photo: "Collars" protect tomato transplants from cutworm damage. JERRY HOWARD/POSITIVE IMAGES. Inset, above: Rooted cuttings and seedlings in a cold frame. MARGARET HENSEL/POSITIVE IMAGES. Inset, opposite page: Glass "tents" are one method of providing extra heat to cold-sensitive plants like lettuce. JERRY HOWARD/POSITIVE IMAGES.

Full-page photo: Nasturtiums are colorful, easy-to-grow, and make good companion plants for many vegetables. ANN REILLY: PHOTO/NATS. **Inset: Petunias in a flower box.** PRISCILLA CONNELL: PHOTO/NATS.

Chapter 6

Controlling Pests and Disease

Keeping Out Unwanted Animals

Your approach to getting rid of unwanted animals in your garden will be determined by your own philosophy and influenced by the appetites of those intruders. If you are concerned about the environment and dislike using poisonous substances or harming animals, your approach to pest control will differ from the person who is intent on having the perfect garden and getting rid of the rascals, no matter what.

The methods you choose may be determined by the amount of time and money you wish to invest. It's a good idea to garden for a while in a particular area to find out just who your enemies are. Identify those animals and birds that are determined to share your garden with you and watch to see which vegetables are most attractive to them. Then you can take steps to repel the culprits and concentrate on protecting specific crops. Unfortunate indeed is the gardener who is attempting to raise vegetables in an area inhabited by all the creatures discussed in the following pages!

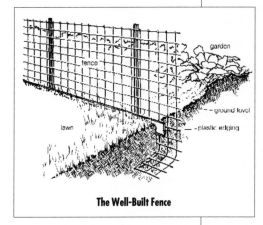

The Well-Built Fence

Gardening can be the most pleasant of avocations, so don't let a few gatecrashers or uninvited guests ruin it for you. Above all, don't give up in frustration. Never forget that man is *supposed* to be the most intelligent of the animals. Surely you can outwit the other critters.

Fencing Around Your Garden

A fenced-in garden generally fares much better than one open to traffic. A fence can keep out the neighbor's dog, your own children, and a few rabbits and cats. But a simple picket or wire fence does not stop everything: Groundhogs and moles dig under them, raccoons and squirrels climb over them, deer hurdle them, slugs ignore them, and birds perch on them while digesting your delicacies. Fences can be expensive, and the barrier designed to keep out absolutely all invaders is not only exorbitant in price but also impractical. However, by investing some time and effort to construct a fence that's burrow-proof, you'll be a lot happier in the long run.

Build your fence in the fall, while the memory of crops unsavored (because the varmint got there first) still stings. Here's how.

Dig a trench 1 foot deep and 1 foot wide around the entire garden and install fencing 5 feet tall or more (stretched on metal fence posts). The fence should be 3 feet or more above ground, with 1 foot below the ground and 1 foot running horizontally underground to discourage burrowing beasts. (See illustration on the previous page.) Fill in

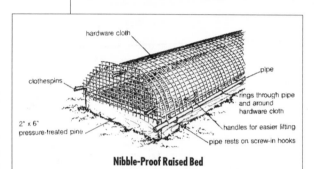

Nibble-Proof Raised Bed

the trench and reseed the lawn if necessary. Around the bottom of the fence, you may want to sink a 4-inch-high plastic edging to keep weeds from growing into the garden.

If you've decided to fence in your garden, but the creation of a gate sounds technical, install a fence with a built-in stile. It's easy to build, beats bending a fence to crawl over it, offers a place to put things, like those dozen tomatoes you just picked, and makes an easy entrance to the garden.

If you till your garden, you'll need an opening that's wide enough to allow garden machinery to pass through. Gates can be complicated to construct. A substitute: On each side of your fence opening, drive two metal fence posts (leaving enough of the posts exposed to equal the height of the fence) so there is a slot between them. The gate is a 3- by 6-foot wooden frame with hardware cloth stretched on it. It slides between the double fence posts like a sliding door — no hinges or latches to fuss with. Just remember to close it when you leave the garden.

NIBBLE-PROOF YOUR RAISED BEDS

Take a few minutes to cover your raised bed to make it nibble-proof. Rig a tunnel of hardware cloth to protect lettuce, spinach, basil, and parsley grown in the bed. Staple the hardware cloth on one side and attach a pipe to the other side to weigh it down. The pipe rests on hooks screwed into the pressure-treated timbers that contain the bed. Handles above the pipes make it easy to lift the mesh to cultivate and harvest. To close in the ends, attach pieces of hardware cloth with clothespins.

GETTING NATURAL HELP WITH INTRUDERS

Why should you be doing all the work? Get help fighting off the intruders the natural way.

■ The family cat prowling the garden will control its population of chipmunks, mice, and young rabbits.

■ Plant daffodils — their bulbs are bitter, so mice and chipmunks won't eat them. If you're determined to have tulips, interplant them with *Fritillaria imperialis* (crown imperial) bulbs. These 2- to 3-foot-tall plants have pendulous red, orange, or yellow blooms, which exude a skunk-like odor that repels rodents and moles.

■ Make a few birdhouses and place them near the garden. Birds will help get rid of unwanted insects. Or spot some simple bird baths here and there in your garden as an enticement to feathered helpers. A house wren feeds 500 bugs and caterpillars to her babies in one afternoon; a brown thrasher consumes thousands of bugs a day.

■ Save fur from brushing and grooming your dog and scatter it in the garden. It deters nibblers and also adds nitrogen to the soil as it decomposes. No dog? Ask the local pet-grooming operation to save fur for you, or try human hair from the barbershop.

■ If you'd rather not share your berries with the birds you've attracted, cover your berry bushes and strawberry beds with used tobacco netting as the fruit begins to ripen. It can be easily lifted when you want to harvest. Or replace the windows in your portable cold frames with screens and set them over ripening strawberry plants.

You can also plant specifically for the birds, so that they'll be less likely to raid cultivated berries. They prefer the tartness of wild fruit, so nurture red and black chokeberries, barberry, wild honeysuckle, autumn olive, Russian olive, mountain ash, staghorn sumac, and mulberry.

■ Ravenous crows can be stopped from pulling up newly planted corn by scattering crow repellent (available at feed stores), either on the bed or mulched loosely with hay after seeding.

■ If you can't keep birds away from your corn, try laying down a 3-foot-wide strip of black plastic with holes in it. Then plant the corn through the holes. The birds don't seem to like walking on the plastic, and your soil will stay warm and speed the growth of the corn. And there's no weeding!

A SHORT LIST OF BENEFICIAL INSECTS

INSECT	BENEFIT
Braconid Wasps	Females lay eggs in the body of the tomato hornworm, which the larvae then consume as their first meal.
Lacewing Fly	Pale green, flylike bug that thrives on aphids.
Calosoma Beetle	Hard-shelled, 2 inches long; expecially loves to eat caterpillars.
Hover Fly	Larvae of this four-winged fly feed on aphids and scale insects.
Ichneumon Fly	Lays eggs in caterpillars and their pupae, which the young flies then consume.
Ladybug	Eats its weight in aphids daily.
Praying Mantis	Up to 3 inches long; feasts on many pests, including mosquitoes.
Spiders	Many species subsist on garden pests.
Wheel Bug	Gray and 1½ inches long, in profile it looks as if a cogged wheel were attached to its back; it preys on soft-shelled pests.

DEALING WITH BUGS AND DISEASE

Most gardeners panic when they see a bug eating and ruining their crops. These folks then rain destruction on their whole garden by spraying to squash out one bug. The better and easier solution is to let the bugs eat — spray only when your crop is really threatened. Insect pests will eventually come into balance with their natural enemies. This will also encourage the population of beneficial creatures, such as birds, bats, toads, snakes, spiders, and ladybugs to eat lots of those pesky bugs and leave you more time for summer fun.

When insects do get ahead of your plants, you'll upset natural balances least if you use a botanically derived insecticide. Rotenone, which comes from the roots of two tropical plants, derris and cubé, has a drawback. Alas, it kills ladybug larvae as well as the bad guys. Pyrethrum, made from the dried flowers of chrysanthemums, spares ladybugs and bees.

BENEFICIAL INSECTS

Lest the entire insect kingdom be given a black eye, it should be noted that several bugs are on your side. Two of these, the ladybug and the praying mantis, can be purchased through some of the larger garden supply houses.

PREVENTIVE MEDICINE

Weekend gardeners don't have the time, energy, or patience to play nursemaid to a crop of sickly plants. If you want to amass a wealth of healthy plants, then you have to invest in preventive gardening practices. Spend more time keeping your plants healthy, instead of wasting your time treating plants that get sick.

There are times when nothing you can do will prevent bug infestations or devastation from disease. Certain plants are more susceptible to pests, while others suffer greatly due to unusual weather conditions. Sometimes the most practical approach to treating severely damaged plants is to simply throw them away.

Knowing when to give up and throw out a sick plant can be difficult. You'll have to consider how much time and energy you are willing to invest, how much you really like the plant, and whether or not the plant's problem is a freak occurrence or one that will return to haunt you year after year.

WAYS TO PREVENT PLANT PROBLEMS

- Keep your garden clean. Tall weeds and overripe flowers attract all sorts of problems. Nip off dead flowers, sweep up your pruning crumbs, and pull out the weeds.
- Water works wonders. A well-watered plant has a strong defense system that wards off many pests. Whenever you let a tree, shrub, or tiny plant feel the stress of thirst, the time becomes ripe for a hostile takeover. Spider mites, aphids, and a host of diseases are all attracted to weak and wilting

37

plant life. Too much water is also an invitation to disaster. Soggy soil encourages disease and fungal infections. Pay attention to the watering needs of your plants.

■ Overfertilizing causes an overabundance of soft green growth. Succulent green growth is more susceptible to frost, insect, and disease damage. Keep your plants well fed, but not overfed. Use a little less chemical fertilizer than the label recommends. Improve your soil with organic matter and you won't have to worry about fertilizing so much with chemicals.

■ Give your plants room to breathe. Good air circulation is especially important in shady, moist sections of your yard. Avoid the overcrowded jungle look. Thin out and throw out overgrown plant life. Opening up the garden also allows the antiseptic rays of the sun to pass through.

■ You can probably avoid 90 percent of your plant problems if you just put the right plant in the right place. Plants that are grown in the soil, weather, and light conditions that they love are plants without problems. Read, research, and remember to ask questions about every plant you consider adding to your garden. Describe your planting spot to the experienced personnel at your local nursery or garden center. Instead of buying a plant and then figuring out where to locate it, choose a location and let them figure out what kind of plant would most like to grow there.

Warning Signs to Watch For

■ **Dropping leaves.** Check for lack of water, mites, or wet and rotten roots. *Treatment:* Wash the plant; dig into the soil to check for dryness or excessive wetness.

■ **Pale coloring or change in leaf color.** Could be sunburn or not enough light. Could also be over- or underfertilization. Mites may be feeding on the back of the foliage. *Treatment:* Check for mites, wash with mild soap; consider fertilizing with a fast-acting liquid food. Add or take away shade.

■ **Bite marks or ragged holes in foliage.** Look for chewing insects like caterpillars or slugs. *Treatment:* Pluck them off.

■ **Shriveled new growth.** Could be disease or lack of water, cold temperatures, or root problems. *Treatment:* Clip off unsightly sections; check for dry soil.

■ **Sticky or sooty black leaves.** Suspect aphids. The sticky stuff is the honeydew they excrete. The black film is just mold growing on the sticky dew. *Treatment:* Hose down trees or wash plants with soapy water.

- **Black or scorched look to the foliage.** Usually some kind of disease. *Treatment:* Clip off damaged sections.
- **Spots, mold, or blotches on the leaves.** All kinds of disease and some types of insects can cause funny leaf spots. *Treatment:* Remove the worst-looking leaves. Clean up debris around the plant. Try to increase air circulation.
- **Plant doesn't grow, looks listless.** Lack of water, lack of nutrients, compacted soil. *Treatment:* Check for dry soil; try a liquid plant food; loosen the soil with shallow cultivation.

Get Tough with Slugs

Slugs are hazards in a mulched garden or in damp soil — and they especially love new seedlings. You may not object to sharing your vegetables with a cotton-tailed rabbit or a cagy raccoon, but it is hard to love a slug. If a poll were to be taken today, slugs would emerge as the Number One enemy of gardeners coast to coast. All garden crops are attractive to slugs. What can you do about them?

- Slugs can't tolerate sharp or caustic materials against their soft bodies. Spread a ½-inch-deep, 6-inch-diameter circle of sharp sand around new seedlings, or try wood ashes, lime, cinders, or diatomaceous earth.

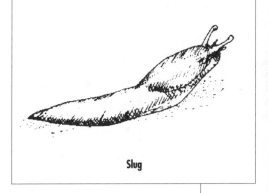

- Pour a "slug" of beer into shallow dishes placed around the garden as slug bait. The slugs will over-imbibe, fall in, and drown.

- Feeling murderous? Stalk slugs in the evening with a salt shaker.

Slug

Sprinkle them twice for insurance sake. You may want to carry the salt shaker in your pocket to be ready whenever a slug appears. Or fill a spray bottle with a solution of half water and half vinegar and spray away.

- Slugs seek cover in the daytime, making them a little easier to catch and kill. Put shingles in the garden as traps, and each morning lift the shingles and kill the slugs gathered underneath them.

Cutworms and Other Annoyances

No gardener wants to replace transplants severed at ground level by cutworms. Protect yours with collars pushed 1 inch into the ground. Make them from: tin cans, with the tops and bottoms removed; paper cups with the bottoms punched out; sections of milk cartons; cardboard; or 2-inch squares of two thicknesses of newspaper placed around each stem.

Scare away the aphids, which are accustomed to the cool, dark undersides of leaves, with plenty of light. Spread a square of aluminum foil under affected plants, and (supposedly) the aphids will be confused by the increased light and leave. Do this around squash plants, too, to repel the squash bug. If you don't get rid of the bugs, the foil will at least act as a mulch to smother weeds and will bounce more light onto crops that need a lot of sun.

If green lacewings invade your garden, do nothing but welcome them. Their larvae are death to aphids.

Interplant white radishes with cucumbers to deter cucumber beetles.

Say Sayonara to Japanese Beetles

Hire your children to save the garden from Japanese beetles — pay them a penny a bug. In the evening, when the beetles won't fly away, the kids can tiptoe along and brush them from plant foliage into jars of kerosene. Meanwhile, you can relax with a good book or take in the evening news.

You can also let a bug trap do all the work — it entices the beetles with a female sex scent combined with a floral lure. Victims are trapped in a bag and die inside from the sun's heat. Replace the bag when it's full. One trap services an area of 5,000 square feet. Be sure to hang it 30 feet downwind of plants you want to protect. If you set it near the plants, it will attract beetles to them.

Planting for Natural Pest Control

Many herbs and flowers are easy to grow and a boon to the gardener who'd just as soon have someone or something else do pest control. Interplant crops with onions, garlic, and marigolds. Try sage, mint, catnip, or dill among your cabbages. Sage, for instance, gives off camphor, which repels the cabbage butterfly. Some plants may discourage insect infestation not only by their specific effects, but by breaking up a large planting of one crop, which is an open invitation to pests.

Companionable Herbs

Herbs	Companions
Basil	Tomatoes. Dislikes rue. Repels flies and mosquitoes.
Borage	Tomatoes, squash, and strawberries. Deters tomato worm.
Catnip	Deters flea beetle.
Chamomile	Cabbages and onions.
Chervil	Radishes.
Chives	Carrots.
Dead Nettle	Potatoes. Deters potato bug.
Dill	Cabbage. Dislikes carrots.
Fennel	Most plants dislike it; plant away from gardens.
Flax	Carrots, potatoes. Deters potato bug.
Garlic	Roses and raspberries. Deters Japanese beetle.
Horseradish	Potato. Deters potato bug.
Hyssop	Cabbage and grapes. Deters cabbage moth. Dislikes radishes.
Marigolds	Plant throughout garden. Discourages Mexican bean beetles, nematodes, and other insects. The workhorse of companion plants.
Mint	Cabbage and tomatoes. Deters white cabbage moth.
Nasturtium	Radishes, cabbage, and cucurbits; plant under fruit trees. Deters aphids, squash bugs, striped pumpkin beetles.
Petunia	Beans.
Pot Marigold	Tomatoes. Deters tomato worm, asparagus beetles, and carrot fly.
Rue	Roses and raspberries. Deters Japanese beetles. Dislikes sweet basil.
Sage	Rosemary, cabbage, and carrots. Dislikes cucumbers. Deters cabbage moth, carrot fly.
Southernwood	Cabbage. Deters cabbage moth.
Summer Savory	Beans and onions. Deters bean beetles.
Tansy	Roses and raspberries. Deters flying insects, Japanese beetles, striped cucumber beetles, squash bugs, and ants.
Thyme	Cabbage. Deters cabbage worm.

CHAPTER 7

HARVESTING AND MORE

Can anything equal the crunch of freshly picked and barely cooked young snap beans, the sweetness of peas and corn rushed from garden to pot, or the wonder of a sun-ripened tomato? We rejoice in their quality, but there are times when even the most avid gardener has been overburdened by their quantity. Many have wished for a hammock or a cool splash in the ocean instead of the endless row of ripe raspberries screaming to be picked right then, always on the hottest July day. And they've wondered, how, by the time they've picked to the end of the row, more berries had uncannily ripened at the beginning?

PICK EARLY, PICK OFTEN

Get them while they're little! This time we mean crops, not weeds. It's not only less work to pick young crops; they also just plain taste better than tough, overmature produce. Regular picking encourages a plant to produce more, so you'll get a better harvest. Small, tender vegetables also require less time and energy to process.

Knowing when vegetables are perfect for picking is a skill that you will gain with gardening experience. In general, though, it is best to bring crops in from the garden just before you are going to eat them or prepare them for storage in the freezer, in a root cellar, or in canning jars. With every minute that passes from the time the produce is picked until the time it is eaten or processed, the vegetables lose quality and food value. Never leave fresh vegetables sitting around for a long time. If, for some reason, you have to pick

MANY HANDS MAKE LIGHT WORK

"The best solution to tedious harvesting chores," says one gardener, "is to have lots of kids! Corral them to shell the peas, cut the beans, husk the corn, and skin the beets."

Lacking a crew of children, plan a social occasion to mesh with the height of raspberry, pea, or bean season. Bill it as a harvesting party, and have a grand time with picking, shelling, and freezing in the same way that folks had with husking bees in times past. It works best with friends who have no garden. Chances are they'll want to take some of that excess harvest home with them.

vegetables some significant time before they are going to be used, keep them either in a refrigerator or in a cool, dark cellar. This will slow down the deterioration process.

Some vegetables can be picked before they are completely mature. Young onions, beets, carrots, cabbages, and the leaves from head-lettuce plants that have not yet had time to form heads are all delicious. You will find that most of the early crops in your garden will mature quite suddenly, and that there is an all-too-short period of time to harvest them before they go by. Later varieties and succession crops are not so frustrating, because they ripen in the fall when the weather is cooler and, because it is cooler, they are not apt to mature so quickly.

If you want your plants to continue bearing vegetables, you must keep them harvested. Pick everything you can as soon as it is ready, even if you know that it is impossible for you to use it all. If you absolutely have to, you can even throw your surplus on the compost pile. Putting unused vegetables back into the garden soil through composting is not nearly so wasteful as throwing them away. Better still, make plans to preserve some of what you have left over, or share some with neighbors and with people in need.

The crops you harvest latest in the season are the easiest and best ones to store. Eat your first plantings of beets and carrots throughout the summer months, and plan to use your later plantings for canning and freezing.

People often boast about having the biggest beets or carrots. This is fine for your ego, if you want something to take to the county fair, but eating these prize-winning monsters can often be like chewing on a piece of old shoe leather. Grow vegetables that are "table size." This means harvesting beets, for example, when they are slightly larger than a lemon. Carrots shouldn't be much bigger around than your thumb. Big, big vegetables have "gone by"; they have passed the point of being ripe, tender, and flavorful.

The more you harvest, the more you grow. If you don't pick your lettuce, it will go to seed. You will probably find that you can cut down the plants about three times before the lettuce gets bitter. Chard and other heat-tolerant greens can be cut continuously all summer long. If you keep cutting spinach, you can get as many as four harvests. Don't forget to cut little leaves, big leaves — the whole works.

Too often, when folks harvest leaf lettuce, they just pick at it. They take off one leaf at a time, picking only the biggest ones. What you should do is take a long knife or scissors and cut the whole row down to a height of about 1 inch. Don't cut down more than you can use at any one time. Keep moving down the row, cutting the lettuce as you need it. By the time you get around to harvesting to the end of the row, you can go back to the beginning and start all over again on the new lettuce that will have then grown back.

Prolonging the Harvest Is Important

Plant early to extend the growing season as much as possible. Grow vegetables as late as you can, too. Plant all of your hardiest crops as soon as the soil can be worked in the spring and again later in the summer for a fall crop.

There are two other ways to prolong your garden's productive period. One is to make several successive plantings of the same vegetable in different parts of the garden. The other method is to sow two or three varieties of the same crop — an early, a mid-season, and a late variety.

You might, for example, plant three different varieties of sweet corn. You will find growing times listed on seed packets or in your favorite catalog. If you choose the right combination of varieties, you can have a second crop ripening at just about the time you have finished harvesting the first. If you sow bush beans and pole beans at the same time, your bush beans will have stopped producing by the time the pole beans are ready.

Believe it or not, a program for a long harvest period begins sometime in the middle of winter, when you should be carefully reading and studying the maturation times of the vegetables you want to plant. If you know the number of days to maturity, you can accurately stagger the harvesting times by selecting the right varieties and by making successive plantings at strategic times.

Chapter 8

Time-Saving Tips and Routines

Becoming a true weekend gardener is a lifelong pursuit; every year you seem to learn more, either from your own gardening experience or from fellow gardeners. The following time-saving tips represent an accumulation of years of secrets from the true gardening pros. Read them — and call them your own!

■ Keep a month-by-month schedule of reminders to make your work in the garden more efficient. In a looseleaf notebook, with a section for each month, list all of the general jobs that need to be done, as well as the care that particular plants will require. A sample entry for April might be:

> **General** — work soil when possible
> **Asparagus** — fertilize and cultivate
> **Currants** — cover with nylon net

The looseleaf format makes it simple to add or change information. This notebook is the perfect place to keep your plot designs with overlays for changes you want to make next year.

■ Stroll around your garden with shears or a knife in your hand and, as you savor the sights, snip off dead blooms and pull out obvious weeds.

■ How many times have you reached the garden, then remembered you forgot the ball of twine or the trowel? How many times have you promised yourself to make a note in your garden notebook, but have forgotten it by the time you reached the house? Stop forgetting! Put up a post at one corner of your garden and mount a mailbox on it. The mailman won't deliver your gardening catalogs there, but you'll find it's a wonderful spot for all your tools, your notebook (don't forget a couple of pens or pencils), a piece of worn sheeting from which to rip pieces to tie up the tomatoes — all those little things essential to gardening.

■ During the winter, put an end to next summer's frantic rummaging — organize your tools. If each one has its own hook in your tool storage area, you will never again waste time searching for it. Pegboard provides a flexible method of storing tools, since you can move hooks around to accommodate new purchases.

- Clean metal parts of spades, shovels, forks, rakes, and hoes with a wire brush, emery cloth, or steel wool. Apply a protective coating of oil with an old cloth. Floor wax will rejuvenate the handles.
- Set up a time-save for next season. Fill an old pail with sand. Pour into it a quart or so of oil (used motor oil is fine) and mix it up a bit. After every use of your hoes, rakes, shovels, and other hand tools, push them into the oily sand a few times. They'll emerge shiny and with a film of oil to keep them from rusting. Your tools will last a lot longer, and you'll never again have to face the dreary job of polishing rust off of them.

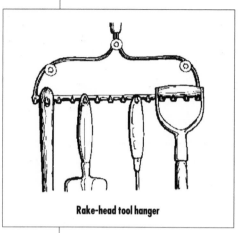

Rake-head tool hanger

- Attach an old rake head to the wall and use it as a hanger for hand tools.
- If you're like many of us, your hoses lie on the garage floor, trampled and tangled, or hang on a single spike, bent and broken. Save the time and money involved in replacing the hose. Drive three spikes into a board so that each spike is one point of a triangle. Cut three short sections of hose from that one you ruined by hanging it over the single spike. Cover the three spikes with sections of hose. Now hang up that new hose — and be proud of it.

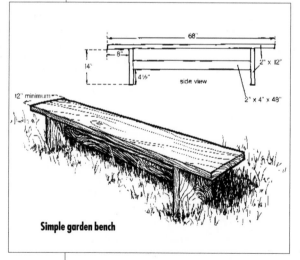

Simple garden bench

- Your garden shouldn't be shaded — but there should be some shade nearby, and this bench should be in it. Build it in two hours, and enjoy it on those warm afternoons when the weeds won't grow much anyway.

Full-page photo: Eggplant is a beautiful and popular vegetable. ANN REILLY: PHOTO/NATS. **Inset: Vegetables and flowers grown together in raised beds.** JERRY HOWARD/POSITIVE IMAGES.

Full-page photo: Cultivating between rows helps keep down the weeds. IVAN MASSAR: PHOTO/NATS. **Inset, top: Transplanting spinach seedlings.** JERRY HOWARD/POSITIVE IMAGES. **Inset, above: Young plants started from seed.** ANN REILLY: PHOTO/NATS.

Full-page photo: A well-kept garden, with phlox, onions, and scarlet runner pole beans. MARGARET HENSEL/POSITIVE IMAGES. **Inset: Adding weeds to the compost pile.** JERRY HOWARD/POSITIVE IMAGES.

Full-page photo: Both flowers and vegetables lend themselves to container growing. JERRY HOWARD/POSITIVE IMAGES. **Inset: A slug devours a yarrow leaf.** ANN REILLY: PHOTO/NATS.

Full-page photo: Freshly cut asparagus. PRISCILLA CONNELL: PHOTO/NATS. **Inset: Harvesting lettuce.** JULIE O'NEIL: PHOTO/NATS.

You need an 8-foot 2" x 12" (or wider) for the seat and legs, and a 4-foot 2" x 4" for a brace. Cut two 14-inch pieces from the plank for legs, leaving a seat area 68 inches long. Center the 2" x 4" brace between the legs, glue with exterior-type glue, and attach with ¼" x 4" countersunk flat-head wood screws. Attach the legs to the seat by gluing and using the same size screws. Stain or finish the bench to suit your own tastes.

25 PLANTING HINTS

1. Soak seeds of beets, Swiss chard, and peas for 15 or 20 minutes before planting. Soak parsley, New Zealand spinach, and celery seed overnight to hasten germination.
2. Make multiple plantings of lettuce.
3. Looseleaf lettuces are quicker and easier to grow than heading types. Plant Romaine lettuce for a crunchy, meatier leaf that does quite well in hot weather.
4. Start seeds of buttercrunch lettuce in beds. Transplant seedlings 8 inches apart in all the empty spaces of the garden — next to the peas, between rows of onions, or between young brassicas.
5. Plant early lettuce between asparagus rows.
6. Having trouble starting lettuce in hot weather? Since it germinates best in cool ground, chill the seed in the refrigerator, plant it, then lay blocks of ice over it, and insulate from the sun with feed bags. Try this with late plantings of spinach or peas, too.
7. Does spinach bolt too soon in your garden? Try New Zealand spinach, which does better in warm weather, or grow Malabar spinach on a fence or trellis.
8. Leaf crops — lettuce, spinach, chard, mustard greens, and parsley — do well in partially shaded locations.
9. Always inoculate your legume seed before planting. You can buy legume inoculant, which looks like black powder, through seed catalogs or from feed stores. It adds a fresh culture of nitrogen-fixing bacteria to the seed, which will increase the yield and quality of peas and beans. Moisten the seeds and shake them with the powder just before planting. A touch of honey on the seeds makes the powder stick better. Keep unused inoculant in the refrigerator until you need it again. There is also a granular type of inoculant that can be sprinkled in furrows as you sow.
10. For earliest peas, prepare the planting trench in the fall, then, in the spring, just push the seed into the soil.
11. Early in the season, till up a 10-foot square of your garden.

Scatter on it one pound of a shorter-bushed pea, such as Little Marvel. Till or rake in the peas, then walk over the soil. And that's it until two months later, when you return to harvest the peas—you should harvest 50 pounds of pods from that tiny space. There's no need for fences or other supports —the peas will support each other.

12. Looking for a vegetable that requires a minimum of effort to grow? Then consider the Jerusalem artichoke. Plant a few tubers in a bed in one corner of your garden, and that's it. They need little or no care — the greatest effort probably goes into keeping them from taking over your entire garden. They'll easily discourage the advances of the hungriest insects. Dig them up in the fall or early spring. You'll miss a few — and they'll grow to provide your crop for the next season. They're delicious and nutritious, fresh or cooked.

Plant corn in blocks to ensure pollination.

13. Lima beans need warm soil. Pre-sprout seeds before planting to reduce the chances of their rotting in the garden. Start them in deep flats in vermiculite or perlite. Limas are an "iffy" crop in the North.

14. For the direct seeding of brassicas without laborious thinning, put sticks in the ground 18 inches apart. Plant a few seeds by each stick. Gradually thin to one plant by snipping off seedlings at ground level. Plant the empty spots between the sticks with lettuce or spinach, which will be harvested by the time the brassicas need more space.

15. Plant collard greens. That way you won't have to do battle in your garden with cabbage worms.

16. Learn to recognize "volunteers." Once you plant dill, you'll never have to plant it again. Let the seeds from a few flower heads scatter each year. Be alert for the feathery green tufts that emerge the following spring and save a few when you cultivate or mulch.

17. Have potatoes without digging. Place seed potatoes 1 foot apart on top of last year's mulch, or on a fall deposit of a few inches of leaves, preferably shredded. Cover with a foot of loose hay. When the tops die down, just rake off the hay. You can even steal a few new potatoes during the season without hurting the plant. Carefully lift the hay when potato blossoms begin to drop, break off tiny potatoes from the mother plant, and then replace the hay.

18. Make sure that onion necks are exposed to the sun and not covered with dirt. By harvest time, they will already be partially dried.

19. Corn takes a lot out of the soil, and it can take a lot out of the gardener, too. To satisfy corn's voracious appetite, dig manure into the soil in the spring and give it booster feedings when it is 8 to 10 inches high and again when silks form.

    Corn is wind-pollinated. The male flower is the tassel, the female flower the silk. Every kernel has a silk attached to it. Undeveloped kernels on a cob mean that they weren't fertilized. To ensure complete pollination, don't plant corn in some long row. Planting in blocks is best. (Refer to the illustration on the previous page.)

20. For cucumber flavor without cucumber vines, plant the annual herb borage or the perennial salad burnet. Mince and add to salads.

21. Stick seeds of winter squash in a partially finished compost pile. The squash plants camouflage the pile, which gives the squashes nourishment and the room they need to sprawl.

22. If you do let winter squash trail, leave a minimum of 5 feet between plants.

23. Interplant a second crop of bush beans between bands of beets and carrots. In a month, all the soil will be shaded and there will be no place for weeds to grow.

24. Plant cucumbers between corn plants to give the cukes some light shade, which they like. Both crops like heat and moisture.

25. Aim for a three-year rotation in your garden, based on the various plants' needs for nutrients.

- **Year One:** Heavy feeders (corn, squash, brassicas, tomatoes, and melons).
- **Year Two:** Heavy givers (legumes, which return nitrogen to the soil—including peas, beans, alfalfa, clover, and vetch).
- **Year Three:** Light feeders (root crops, such as beets, onions, carrots, turnips, kohlrabi, and parsnips).

Or interplant the three types of crops in the same bed.

THE 15 EASIEST VEGETABLES TO GROW

Beans	Cucumbers	Peppers
Beets	Kale	Radishes
Cabbage	Lettuce	Spinach
Carrots	Onions	Tomatoes
Corn	Peas	Zucchini

THE 15 EASIEST ANNUALS TO GROW

Calendula	Gloriosa Daisy	Petunia
Candytuft	Impatiens	Phlox
Celosia	Lobelia	Portulaca
Coleus	Marigold	Salvia
Forget-Me-Not	Nasturtium	Sweet Alyssum

Chapter 9

Hassle-Free Lawn Care

The perfect lawn has become an American obsession. Every homeowner want a deep green lawn free of weeds and clover and kept as short and uniform as a new pile carpet. The suburban dream of a perfect lawn has created a high-maintenance nightmare.

The all-American, all-uniform, and always perfect lawn just isn't natural. Uniform fields of grass are contrary to what nature had in mind when she planted that first prairie of waving grass and wildflowers. If you plan to enjoy gardening, stop trying to conquer Mother Nature and start cooperating with her. Free yourself from turf-care torture by realizing the evils of the perfect lawn.

The Drawbacks of a Perfect Lawn

Here are three reasons to stop striving for a perfect lawn:

1. **It's a time-consuming task.** If you stop mowing long enough to think about it, would any gardener waste time on a tree or shrub that demanded weekly pruning? Mowing the perfect lawn is without a doubt the most time-consuming part of owning a patch of grass. The problem stems from the fact that the image of the "perfect lawn" in many neighborhoods is a shortly cropped lawn; a lawn that barely skims the 1 inch mark on a ruler. Some lawn fanatics will waste time mowing twice a week to achieve this close-cropped look.

   These lawn-lovers need to lighten up and lengthen their lawn along with their free time. A super short lawn consumes more water, more fertilizer, and — worst of all — more time to keep it healthy.
2. **You're wasting energy on weeds.** Vowing to keep every weed out of your lawn is the fastest way to break a promise. Commit yourself to a weed-free lawn and you'll be wasting precious energy on a treadmill task. Energy that could be better spent working with your more grateful, more productive, and more beautiful flowers and shrubs.
3. **Money is the root of all evil in maintaining the perfect lawn.** Maintaining the perfect lawn requires large amounts of water and fertilizer. Not only are water and lawn fertilizers expensive and time-consuming to apply, but this overindul-

gence of your lawn may come at the expense of the rest of your garden. A greedy lawn demanding constant chemicals and special equipment to keep it near perfection is an enormous burden on any gardening budget.

Starting a New Lawn from Seed

Let's get the bad news over with first. There's no real shortcut for starting a lawn from seed. After preparing the soil and sowing the seed, you must commit yourself to keeping the seedbed constantly moist for several weeks. Dry soil is the most common cause of seeding disaster. Console yourself with the thought of all the money you're saving. Sprinkling seed is still the cheapest way to start a new lawn.

■ **Don't skimp on grass seed.**

The most expensive grass seeds are the newer named varieties that have been bred for better performance and disease resistance. These hybrid seeds cost more, but are definitely worth it. For example, instead of reading "perennial ryegrass," the label on the package of seed should bear the name of a particular variety, such as "Manhattan perennial ryegrass."

■ **Use a pre-mixed combination of grass types.**

Don't plant a lawn of all bluegrass or all ryegrass in an attempt at a unified look. Increase your odds of at least one of the grasses doing well by planting for some variety. A lawn composed of just one type of seed is more susceptible to total wipeout from insects or disease.

Also, don't use up all your seed the first time you plant. Save out some seed for going over the bare spots later on.

Bury Your Hose for Easy Watering

An efficient and hassle-free method for watering your lawn involves simply running your garden hose over to that sunny slope or side lawn that is always thirsty. Keep the hose hidden by running it alongside the edge of the lawn bordering the flower bed. Now cover the hose (a ½-inch topping of bark or soil is enough to hide it). Leave enough uncovered hose at the end so you can pull it out of hiding when watering is necessary — just a foot or two coiled up under a shrub, easy to drag out when you need it. Better yet, leave the sprinkler hooked up to the hose and hide the whole unit behind a low shrub, close to the lawn. This hidden hose trick will save you the job of coiling and uncoiling the hose all summer.

You can eliminate the irritation of attaching the hose to the faucet all summer long by attaching a double-headed Siamese faucet head to your outlet. These exotic-sounding faucets are cheap and easy to find at any hardware store. Put one on every faucet. Now you can still fill water cans or attach a second hose for filling the pool or watering the dog. Meanwhile, the buried hose stays in place all summer long, ready to deliver water with a minimum of hassle.

Use a Big Sprinkler

The oscillating sprinkler is the best bet for the weekend gardener, because the back-and-forth action of this sprinkler will cover a lot of area. Be sure to run it at full force, so that the water will reach the flowers and shrubs that border your lawn as well. Since you're going to water, you might as well water everything within reach.

Watering Worries Not to Worry About

- Don't worry that watering at night will give your grass a disease. It rains at night, doesn't it? Set your sprinklers to come on in the wee hours of the morning. This is when you get the best water pressure. Early morning watering also keeps your children and pets dry.

- Don't worry that watering on a sunny day will scorch your grass. Pesticides and chemical fertilizers give lawns that scorched look, not watering on a hot day. Watering in the sun is not very efficient, however, since some of the moisture gets sapped up by the heat.

- Don't worry that your brown-looking lawn is dead if watering restrictions during a drought are imposed. Most grass types will just go dormant during a time of water rationing and then spring back to life in the fall.

Water Deeply — and Water Less Often

If you're going to go to all the trouble of turning on a watering system, then, for your lawn's sake, water deeply. Let the sprinkler run until the top 3 to 4 inches of soil are saturated. That way you won't have to think about watering again for days or even weeks. Less frequent but deep watering is not only easier for the lazy lawn grower, but it's better for the health of your lawn. If you water shallowly, the lawn's roots will remain close to the surface, trained to expect their frequent fix of water. But water deeply, letting the sprinkler remain on until the water soaks down half a foot or more, and those roots will follow the moisture way down into the depths of your soil. Once down deep, those grass roots will figure out how to extract moisture from the soil on their own. The longer you water, the longer you can go without watering again. Some soils require overnight watering to saturate them. In other neighborhoods, two hours of watering may be enough. Jab a knife into your soil. If the top 6 inches aren't dark with moisture, keep on watering.

DECIDING WHEN TO WATER

Never waste water. To figure out when it's time for another deep soaking, just step on your lawn. If the grass springs back from your footprint quickly, then things are okay. But if your footprint sticks around, leaving an impression in the grass, you had better start up the sprinklers.

Most lawns can survive a dry summer with a once-a-week watering session. The secret is to run the sprinkler for at least two hours every time you water the lawn. Leave the sprinkler on all night long if that's what it takes to fully wet the top 6 inches of soil. Hard-packed clay soils have trouble absorbing water, and sandy soils have trouble retaining water. Rich, loamy soil can go the longest between waterings.

THE BEST SIZE FOR ANY LAWN

Set your sprinkler in the middle of your lawn. Now turn it on high. The area that gets wet is all the grass you really need. If your sprinkler can't quite reach the corners of your lawn, then trust in fate. What can't be watered easily wasn't meant to be lawn. Replace those outer limits of lawn with drought-resistant groundcover plants or a gravel mulch instead.

WEED WARS

CUTTING THROUGH THE CONFUSION

Forget the sprays, the spreaders, the chemicals, and all the warnings printed on all those label instructions. There is a simple way to kill weeds. Just grab a screwdriver and dig out what you don't want in your lawn.

If this sounds like too much work, consider how much lawn you could hand-weed in the time it takes to drive to a garden center, purchase a product, read about it, and then apply it to your lawn. Consider that some weed killer may drift onto your flowers. Consider the weather and wind conditions, which have to be just right for the chemical weed killers to work. Consider that you may be warned to stay off your lawn for 24 hours after using some weed-killing chemicals. Cut out the chemicals, and your children and pets can eat the lawn if they want. Cut out the weeds, and you can eat a lot of them, too.

SMOTHER THE WEEDS WITH SEEDS

Reseed your lawn each fall or spring to get a chokehold on some of the weeds. Just rake in a little peat moss or topsoil and sprinkle grass seed on top. Do this right before it rains. The thicker your lawn, the thinner the weed supply.

MOWING MATTERS

MOW WEEKLY, BUT MOW IN MINUTES

Grow yourself a smaller lawn. Don't grow it on a slope, under low-hanging tree branches, or with any crazy corners. Only grow as much lawn as you can cut in a half hour.

HOW CLOSE TO MAKE THE CUT

- Avoid the short-cropped lawn. A lawn mowed very short belongs on a golf course, where they plant a special type of grass that can tolerate the torture. Most northern lawns contain some Kentucky bluegrass, and bluegrass hates to be mowed any shorter than 1½ inches.
- You can adjust the mower blades for an even higher cut in the summer, so the longer grass can shade the soil. When the soil is shaded, your lawn requires less water.
- For lawns in the North, just set the blades so they'll cut at 1½ inches all year long.
- To measure how high your mower cuts, set it on cement. Then use a ruler to measure the distance from the ground to the cutting blade.
- Southern lawns can be cut closer. If you live where the snow never falls, then your lawn mix may include a lot of warm-season grasses like Bermuda, or even Dichondra, which is not technically a grass at all, but a tropical perennial herb. These lawns can be mowed very short. Set your mower height at ½ inch all year long. St. Augustine, centipede, and zoysia grasses should all be cut higher, though — more like northern lawns.
- If you're trying to grow grass in a shady area, leave it 2 or even 3 inches long. It needs that extra leaf area to absorb the tiny bit of solar energy that comes its way.

- Leave the grass clippings right where they are if you have a large lawn or use a riding mower. They will dry up and slip into the soil, returning about a third of their nitrogen to the lawn.
- Collect the clippings if you're a lawn fanatic or if your lawn is small. You'll get a tidier look, and the grass clippings will come in handy. The lazy way is to use a bag that attaches right to your mowing machine. Empty the bag into a wheelbarrow that you've parked nearby.
- Always collect the clippings if you mow during cool, rainy weather. Fungal disease moves in when wet globs of matted grass lie around. In shady areas, these matted grass clippings will encourage moss. When grass clippings congregate in clumps, get out the rake and start collecting.

IF YOU HAVE A GIGANTIC LAWN TO MOW

- Forget about using a push mower (which gives a cleaner cut) until you scale down your lawn.
- Invest in a riding mower.
- Pay a lawn service or neighborhood kid to mow your lawn for you.
- Use a power mower that covers the widest section of lawn in one sweep.

- Have a designated dumping spot that's easy to get to. Hide it behind a bush or low fence.
- Grass clippings can be composted by layering them with leaves and soil. Spread a tarp on top of the pile to keep away the flies.
- You can dump grass clippings in a wild section of the yard to smother the weeds.
- If you have the room, spread your clippings all around your trees, shrubs, and flowers. Use a very thin layer, so the cut grass can dry out before it has a chance to mat down.

- If you have extra-long grass to cut, the clippings will fill up your bag quickly. Divide the job into two jobs instead. Mow one day and let the long clippings dry in the sun. Rake the next day, and the clippings will be lighter and much easier to handle.

CHAPTER 10

BULBS FOR CAREFREE COLOR

Formal, fancy, and flagrantly colorful flowers grow from bulbs. Bulbs can give you beautifully simple blooms in all the pastel colors of spring tulips. Bulbs can also dazzle the yard with the vibrant oranges and yellows of summer-blooming gladioluses and begonias.

Once you plant a bulb, the work is over. There's no need to water, feed, or prune back a hearty bulb in bloom. Just think of the bulb as the underground supply center for the flower. The food for that flower is already stored in the bulb. All that you have to do is dig a hole, plant, and wait. Bulbs are nature's very own ready-to-go, pre-fertilized, and pre-measured flower growing kit.

Choose only those bulbs that are easy to grow in your soil and climate. The easy way to research this is to see what pops up in your neighbor's yard. Some bulbs like grape hyacinths and windflowers spread and multiply so easily that, if you admire them aloud, you'll probably get sent home with a freshly dug clump of your own. Gardeners are generous with easy-to-grow plants.

For maximum ease, plant only hardy bulbs that can stay in the ground all winter. Tender bulbs that bloom in the summer, like dahlias, tuberous begonias, and gladioluses, demand more attention. These tender bulbs need to be dug up and stored each fall before the ground freezes. Summer bloomers may also need fertile soil and more water than spring bloomers, which are winter-hardy and easier to ignore. The bulbs that bloom in the spring are also more likely to *naturalize*. This means they will return without replanting each year, and will eventually multiply into large colonies. A single bulb that likes the feel of your garden can grow into a large clump of carefree blooms after only a couple of years.

WHEN TO PLANT BULBS

If you want flowers in the spring (tulips, daffodils, hyacinths, etc.), then plant the bulbs in the fall.

If you need summer color, then plant the bulbs of gladioluses, tuberous begonias, and dahlias in the spring. These bulbs don't care for freezing weather, so plant them after the last spring frost.

If you don't get around to researching what to plant when, just walk into a garden center when you get the urge to plant a few things in the ground. You'll see a display of bulbs set up with pictures of the flowers that will bloom. Bulbs are sold by your local garden center at the time of the year when they should be planted. Go ahead and get carried away. Plant a little bit of everything the first year, so you can judge for yourself what does best in your yard. You're sure to get flowers from just about any bulb the first year you plant it. It's only if you want bulbs that will naturalize and return year after year that you have to be choosy about what you plant.

You'll find plenty of free and accurate planting information at your local garden center or in any mail-order catalogue that sells bulbs.

THE EASY WAY TO PLANT BULBS

- Sort your bulbs into groups of 7 to 12. All the bulbs in each group should be the same type and same color. Use large plastic sandwich bags to keep the groups separate.
- You can skip the sorting stage if you buy your bulbs in presorted packages. Bulbs are often sold in packs of 25 at garden centers.
- Use a big shovel, not a tiny trowel, and dig one community hole for each group of bulbs. One hole for the yellow daffodils, another hole for the red tulips, etc.
- Go ahead and cheat if you don't feel like planting the bulbs as deep as it recommends on the package. If you live where the winters are mild, you can get away with planting your tulips and daffodils 4 to 5 inches deep rather than the 8 to 12 inches that is usually recommended.
- If you need the extra winter protection of deeply planted bulbs but don't feel like digging a hole a foot deep, you can get away with digging a shallow hole, but only if you mound extra soil or leaves 3 or 4 inches thick on top of the planting area. A mulch of fallen leaves makes a wonderful bulb blanket. Pile a little soil on top to keep the leaves in place.
- Once you've got your hole dug, check out the soil. Bulbs will rot in wet and soggy ground. If you have sticky, wet, or clayey soil, add peat moss and sand to the planting hole. If improving wet soil is too much of a bother, then don't waste your time planting bulbs in the ground at all. Pot them up in containers or build raised beds with sandy soil instead. Don't even try to argue with Mother Nature on this point. Bulbs insist on well-drained soil.

■ You may have read that bulbs needs bonemeal or fertilizer mixed into the soil at planting time. You can skip this step. All the food your bulb needs to flower the first year is already stored inside of it. Gritty bonemeal and special bulb foods are fine, but you will still get lovely blooms without fertilizing — for the first year, at least.

■ Once the hole is dug, dump all the bulbs of one group into the community hole, No need to get on your hands and knees yet. Just lean on your shovel as you toss the bulbs from your plastic bag.

■ Now you can squat and arrange the bulbs so that they're all sitting on their bottoms. Space them far enough apart, so that they don't spend the winter rubbing shoulders with one another. You may have to widen the hole a bit at this time. The experts will tell you to leave a 3- to 6-inch space between each bulb, but that means you would have to dig a bigger and wider hole. You can plant them closer and get away with it.

■ Fill in the hole with the soil, but reverse the order when you fill. Put the rich, dark topsoil into the hole first so that this will be closest to the bulbs' roots. What was on top should now be on the bottom. Spread mulch on top of the soil if you need the extra protection from freezing winters or a shallow planting.

■ Don't water, don't worry — just wait. If Mother Nature intends for bulbs to bloom in your yard, then you'll see success the very first year.

MORE MANEUVERS FOR MAXIMUM IMPACT

Here's how to design with various kinds of bulbs to get the maximum return on your energy investment:

■ Plant different types of bulbs, close to one another, but use the same colors to make a bold statement. A clump of yellow daffodils and a dozen golden tulips multiply the color magic. Try pink hyacinths with pink tulips. For maximum impact, make sure your color partners bloom at the same time.

■ Use two or three groups of bulbs, but use only two contrasting colors. Red and yellow tulips or purple and white crocuses stand out more vividly than a huge collection of pastels. Put blue grape hyacinths with your yellow daffodils.

■ Put the early spring bloomers close to the house or along the path you take every day to your car or mailbox. The low-growing crocus and snowdrop bulbs are better appreciated up close.

- Look out your favorite window and focus on a place for spring bulbs. Rainy spring days may keep you indoors, so plan ahead for a blooming view.
- Plant tall tulips and other floppy flowers where they'll be protected from the wind. Situating them between two large shrubs or against a wall is a smart choice.
- Use tiny, delicate bulbs in containers or window boxes, where they'll be closer to eye level. Miniature daffodils in the spring and dwarf dahlias in the summer look just right in small pots or blooming in shallow window boxes.
- Bulbs planted against a solid background won't get lost in a busy landscape. A fence or evergreen shrub makes a fine background for showing off tall tulips or glads. Low growers like dwarf tulips or crocuses stand out near a piece of pavement or patio for contrast.
- Any place where there's a large rock emerging from the ground is a perfect spot for a clump of bulbs. The smooth texture and light color of a boulder magnifies the delicate beauty of your bulb blooms. Use lots of rocks and boulders in your yard's design, and you'll have lots of places to tuck in a few bulbs.
- Summer-blooming bulbs like dahlias and gladioluses that grow tall are easiest to grow alongside a fence — use sticks or stiff wire to prop them up against the fence when they bloom.

Easy-to-Grow Tulips

Tulips are the world's favorite of all spring-blooming bulbs, but time-conscious gardeners must choose wisely to get the most color for the least effort and upkeep.

- The shorter, the better. Low-growing tulips are tidier, since they don't flop over in the wind or from spring rainstorms. Dwarf tulips are also more resistant to summer drought.
- Many low-growing tulips bloom early in the spring, when you really need the color. Lots of shrubs are outblooming each other with flowers in May, but choose a March-blooming tulip and it will have the stage all to itself.
- More than any other reason, choose short-stemmed tulips because they multiply, naturalize, and return each spring more dependably than tall ones.
- Low-growing or dwarf tulips have many different common and scientific names, but all were meant to spend their lives reblooming every spring.

Try planting these five bulbs for many happy returns. They naturalize easily and will rebloom year after year, even if ignored.

Daffodil: The smaller varieties that bloom in clusters, or the hardier types commonly called narcissus are the daffodils that are easiest to naturalize. These easy-growing varieties also bloom earlier in the spring then the taller, showier daffodils.

Autumn Crocus: If your yard looks rather drab in autumn, tuck a few bulbs of a fall-blooming crocus around shrubs and in borders. The spring-blooming crocuses are also bulbs for the weekend gardener. Both types of crocus are planted in the fall and, because the bulbs are small, you don't have to dig a very deep hole. Just bury the crocus bulbs 3 inches deep and you'll have years of dependable blooms.

Hardy Anemone blanda: Sometimes called "windflower," these spring-blooming bulbs will grow in any soil as long as it is well drained. They multiply rapidly. The best thing about this plant is the foliage. The leaves are low, dainty, and compact, so when the flowers die back, you still have a month or two of green groundcover.

Hardy Cyclamen: This is another bulb that will bloom during the autumn or very early spring. These are exotic-looking creatures and closely resemble the delicate florist's cyclamen. The difference is that the hardy cyclamen will survive in dry, rocky soil and spread naturally into larger clumps. The pink-blooming cyclamen blooms in the spring and autumn and even thrives in the crummy soil under evergreen trees. The hardy cyclamen does not need winter protection in mild winter climates. Like the windflower, it has low-growing, attractive foliage.

> ## NAMES TO LOOK FOR WHEN SEEKING EASY-TO-GROW TULIPS
>
> Rock Garden Tulips
> Species Tulips
> Greig Tulip *(Tulipa Greigii)*
> Waterlily Tulip *(Tulipa Kaufmanniana)*
> Foster Tulip *(Tulipa Fosterana)*
>
> **Note:** The height of these tulips will be 4 to 12 inches. (Traditional tulips grow up to 20 inches in height.)

Wood Hyacinth or Scilla: These are the spring-blooming bluebells that grow wild in many parts of the country. Plant a couple bulbs and forget about them. You'll have a lifetime of blue blossoms. These are taller than the more purple grape hyacinths, but the two are often confused because they share the same easy-going temperament and an uncontrollable urge to reproduce themselves. Watch out, though. Given ideal conditions, either of these bulbs can take over your entire lawn and garden and turn into uncontrollable weeds.

Chapter 11

Easy Annuals and Roses

It's flowers that turn a yard into a garden. Food for the soul and blossoms for the bud vase, flowers inside or outside transform a house into a home.

The problem for the weekend gardener is that growing flowers takes a bit more time and energy than maintaining a tree or tending the shrubbery. The maintenance of your flower beds can still be kept to a minimum if you choose the flowering plants carefully. The blooming borders of your dreams don't have to turn into the high-maintenance monsters of your nightmares. You can have your flowers and free time, too.

The rules are the same for flowers as for anything else that grows in your low-maintenance garden:

- Discover which plants bloom easily in your yard and plant lots of them.
- Get ideas from the flowers that do well in your neighbors' gardens. Property close to yours will have similar soil and weather. When you happen upon a flowering plant that does well, reward it by planting more. A mass planting is more impressive than a hodgepodge of different flowers, anyway.
- Don't fight Mother Nature. If wild foxgloves or wood violets spring up uninvited, don't weed them out right away. Welcome any flowering plant that appeals to you. What you should be weeding out are the flowering failures that looked great in the catalogue or garden center, but do nothing but demand attention in your yard.
- Grow the flowers that you really love. It's not work to grow a plant you really love, It's just an enjoyable hobby. Fall in love with a flower and you'll find the time to love the labor.

Good Places to Add Annuals

Bordering the lawn. If you outline the lawn with flowers that sprawl a little, you won't have to worry about edging the grass. Petunias are a good choice because they bloom even better if you nick them with the lawn mower. The floral colors will stand out against the green background of the grass, and the flowers will get watered whenever you soak the lawn.

Plant a flower bed along a pathway. The path to the front door is the obvious place to show off a little fancy floral work. A pathway garden also means that the flowers will be close and convenient for you to putter around in. You could even pull a few weeds or snip a few blossoms every time you step out the front door.

Add a flower bed where it can be viewed from inside. The view that you see when sitting in your favorite chair or eating your supper should be a beautiful blooming scene. Plant large, tall flowers like snapdragons or sunflowers, or masses of flowers like marigolds and impatiens that are easy to see from a distance.

Plant on terraced slopes or above retaining walls and rockeries. Not only will these spots have the good drainage that flowers love, but creeping and cascading blooms really show off when allowed to tumble over a barrier.

Interplant some blooming annuals amongst the vegetables or bordering the vegetable garden. Chances are this is one part of your yard that already has good soil and that gets watered and fertilized regularly. Pansies are an example of an annual that will bloom early, when the vegetable garden is still sparse in the spring. Pluck the pansy blossoms and add them to your salads when you're outside harvesting lettuce.

Deck out the patio with plants, and plant more flowers near the deck. Flowers surrounding your outdoor sitting rooms will be close enough for you to enjoy and yet convenient enough to tend to.

The best place of all. Plant your flowers in pots. A container garden near the front door to greet visitors and pots on the patio to decorate the backyard. For more information on container gardening, see Chapter 12.

Places to Avoid Planting

Don't plant under large trees or next to huge shrubs. Unless you add a 3-inch layer of topsoil or compost, your little flowers will be competing with giant roots for food and water. They'll lose the battle.

Don't plant on the side of the house that nobody ever sees. That's usually the side without any windows. Out of sight means out of control and outrageously high maintenance. Plant shrubs in these landscaping outposts instead.

Don't plant up close to the house under the eaves. Not only is the soil dry and lousy next to cement foundations, but the flower bed won't be seen from inside the house. Do you ever gaze out a window and look straight down? An exception is the front of the house, where you'll want to create a nice public garden. That way, you'll see the flowers as you drive up to the house.

Don't be tempted into adding a flower border alongside a narrow driveway. If the foot traffic doesn't beat the plants down, the wandering wheels will.

Weekend gardeners shouldn't plant "secret gardens" of annual flowers on the outskirts of their property. A distant flower garden will be inconvenient to water and feed when it's too far away from the hub of things to enjoy.

Keep your flowers out of the path of children or pets. Large roaming dogs and children's games are not compatible with a ground-level flower bed. Don't try an island of flowers in the middle of a lawn if you have people and paws romping about.

ANNUALS THE EASY WAY — STARTED TRANSPLANTS

Annual flowers that are sold in little plastic trays as young green plants are sometimes called *bedding plants* or *started transplants*. They got their name because they're often set into the ground 5 or 6 inches apart and soon grow together to form solid beds of blooms.

Here are ten of the easiest-to-grow annuals that are commonly sold as started transplants. Most are sold four to six plants to a pack, with the exception of the geranium starts, which are usually sold as single plants, often in 4-inch pots.

FOR SUNNY SPOTS

Marigold: A dependable bloomer and tolerant of lousy soil, marigolds are always a good investment, so long as you have a sunny spot to grow them in. The short varieties are called French marigolds, and they're easier to grow than the taller African marigolds. Hot weather doesn't bother marigolds, but lack of water does. Very easy to grow from seed, but the started transplants are cheap and available everywhere. Marigolds come in warm yellow and orange colors.

Geranium: Large flowers heads and circular leaves give this plant a dignified, formal look that's perfect for pots or borders in the front yard. Just make sure that the soil drains well and the sun shines on your geraniums for at least half a day, and you won't have any problems. In mild winter climates, your geraniums may return for an encore performance, just like a perennial flower. Bloom colors are sizzling hot reds and oranges or soft salmons and pinks.

Petunia: The easiest way to get massive displays of flowers is to plant petunias. Petunias will even perform in arid desert climates if planted in the spring and fall. They love the sun, but can also bloom beautifully in a partly shaded bed. Buy young plants when choosing petunia starts, and avoid skinny transplants already in bloom or bud. Pinch off the top inch of the plants after transplanting them to encourage bushy side growth. The double-flowering petunias are harder to grow than the single or grandiflora petunias; trailing petunias work wonderfully in hanging baskets.

Alyssum: Low-growing and covered with tiny blossoms, alyssum is the perfect edging or border plant for the weekend gardener. There is sometimes a problem getting them out of their plastic packs and into the soil at their new home. Alyssum hates to be moved, so buy young plants without any blooms and water them well the night before you attempt the transplant. Keep as much soil around the roots of the new plants as you can when you transplant. Alyssum is another sun-loving plant that will adapt and bloom in a lightly shaded spot in the garden. The white variety seems the most vigorous, but alyssum also comes in rose, shades of purple, and a reddish color.

Snapdragon: An old-time favorite that has been bred with better disease resistance, allowing it to qualify as a flower for the weekend gardener. The tall-growing varieties are great for the back of a blooming border; when you cut off the blooming spikes for indoor use, you'll be encouraging more flowers to form. Snapdragons will return (winter over) in mild climates, especially if you plant them close to the house in a protected spot. Look for young transplants, and don't crowd them any closer than 6 inches apart when you set them out in the bed. Most snapdragons won't need staking, and they come in a pastel mix of colors.

Zinnia: Zinnias have always been colorful sun lovers that also love hot summers, but now the dwarf varieties can be easily transplanted from packs. Pinch off the top flower bud as soon as it forms to encourage bushy plants. Don't even try to grow a zinnia in a partially shaded spot and, when you water, avoid wetting the foliage. If you have to fight mildew on your zinnia plants, then say good-bye and plant another annual more tolerant of your moist climate.

For Shady Spots

Impatiens: This annual prefers a little shade, and will bloom even in very deep shade. Frosty weather and dry soil are the two killers of impatiens, so don't plant them outside too early and keep the watering can handy. One of the nicest things about impatiens is the way it cleans up after itself. The dead flowers just fall from the plants all on their own, so you don't have to spend time nipping and clipping these nicely shaped plants. If you buy impatiens plants that are a little bit tall and leggy, snip off the top half of the plants before you put them in the ground. Put the cuttings in a glass of water; after a few inches of roots form, you can plant the cuttings outside.

Lobelia: The annual form of lobelia tolerates both sun and deep shade, and this is one annual that really excels in cool summer climates. Lobelia comes in a trailing form that is perfect for cascading over the edges of pots and rockeries; compact varieties can be grown as an edging plant. Lobelia comes in light blue, dark blue, and blue and white combinations. No snipping of dead flowers is necessary, but you may need to cut these annuals in half around August to keep them blooming until frost.

Wax Leaf Begonia: This is another shade-tolerant flower that doesn't need constant pinching and picking to keep it clean and compact. There are also tuberous begonias, but they are more difficult to grow. The easiest-to-grow begonia has a waxy-looking leaf and small but numerous flowers. The foliage of this annual is often more colorful than the flowers. Wax leaf begonias are often sold as single plants in large 4-inch pots, much like geraniums.

Pansies: These annuals will extend your blooming season because they flower earlier than the other started transplants you can buy. A little frost won't hurt your pansies, so put them in the ground when your daffodils start to bloom. A cool, moist soil supports the greatest number of pansy blooms, but you'll need to protect these tender flowers from slugs and snails.

Picking Out Prime Plants

When confronted with a greenhouse full of plants, you need a few guidelines to help you weed out the weaklings:

■ Short and fat, not tall and skinny is the best shape for young bedding plants to be in. You want to look for squatty plants that will transplant easily into your soil.

■ Look for green plants, but don't chicken out if the plants you want look a little pale. Young plants start to turn pale from lack of light very quickly. Bedding plants that sit on the bottom of a display rack or in the shade of a storefront will green up quickly once you get them home and into the sunshine.

■ Bigger is not always better. Bedding plants are often sold six to each plastic pack, and the older, larger plants are the ones that have been sitting around the longest. These overgrown plants could very well be rootbound — the roots so crowded and tangled that they may not survive a transplant.

■ The bigger the pot, the bigger the value. A new trend at garden centers is to sell single plants in bigger 4-inch pots. The roots aren't crowded together, and the plant can actually grow to blooming size and still survive a transplant. These big plants are perfect for a gardener with more money than time to spend. You can easily fill a few pots on the patio or create a color spot in your yard with these instant flowers. Impatient gardeners will love the idea of setting out plants already in bud or bloom. Just make sure you harden them off for one or two days before introducing them to the great outdoors.

No-Fuss Roses

The easiest-to-grow roses for the weekend gardener are those that adapt well to whatever nature dishes out. The best roses for laid-back gardeners are the old-fashioned species roses, the hardy polyanthas, the floribundas, and disease-resistant shrub roses. The time-conscious gardener must be very picky about rose varieties, or he or she may be burdened with a very picky rose.

The Top Five Low-Maintenance Roses

Shrub Roses: Bonica and Simplicity are the names of two shrub roses that get high marks for low care. Both of these roses will grow to 5 feet in height, and both bloom pink. They are covered with blossoms for most of the summer. Either would make a great hedge.

Polyantha Roses: The Fairy is the favorite low-growing rose of the lazy gardener. Like all polyanthas, The Fairy is adorned with small but numerous flowers, borne in clusters on short stems. This rose stands out from the rest because of its high disease resistance and dainty pink flowers that reappear all summer long.

Hearty Climbers: Improved Blaze wins the prize as the hottest rose ever to ramble over a split-rail fence. Blaze is a climbing red rose that has been improved by modern rose breeders for a longer blooming season. Blaze can be easily trained to cascade over an arbor. Climbing Peace and Climbing Double Delight are two other hard-to-kill climbing roses.

Species Roses or Old-Fashioned Roses: These are closely related to the wild roses that survive on total neglect in the fields. Some don't bloom for as long as modern roses, but many offer the bonus of winter color with bright red rose hips, or seedpods. These roses are so hardy and vigorous that they are sometimes used as a groundcover. They do especially well when allowed to cascade over a sunny hillside. *Rosa rugosa* is a species that survives almost anywhere, even near the seashore, where it blooms in spite of sandy soil and saltwater spray.

Floribunda Roses: This family of roses gives you lots of small flowers that bloom in clusters. Europeana is a good example of an easy-care floribunda, as this rose grows short and bushy. Europeana blooms heavily, and its flowers are a classic rose-red color. Not only does this rose resist disease, but it is also tolerant of very cold and very warm weather conditions. A tidy rose with an easy-going nature.

The favorite varieties mentioned above should not deter you from trying some of the other roses in the same family. Most of the polyantha, floribunda, species, and shrub roses are easy to grow. In your area there may be an even better variety choice than the examples given. Just remember that the easiest-to-grow roses are not the formal hybrid teas with their long stems and gigantic blooms.

Hybrid Tea Roses

The hybrid tea rose is the long-necked beauty that many weekend gardeners only dream about. This is the rose variety that blooms most of the summer with full-sized flowers that are perfect for cutting and displaying in a bud vase.

The tea rose is indeed a gorgeous specimen, improved by plant breeders until it has become the aristocrat of garden flowers. But the hybrid tea rose has been bred for beauty, not brains. This lovely-looking plant has a gluttonous appetite for food and water, and it attracts pests and diseases faster than other, more common, plants. Some hybrid tea roses even have snobbish attitudes to match their fancy bloodlines; they need constant attention to avoid falling victim to one disaster after another.

Despite all their drawbacks, the forewarned gardener can still enjoy a formal rose garden of hybrid tea roses. You must only promise to be particular when you choose these picky roses. Skip over descriptive phrases like "bicolored," "fragrant," and "spellbinding color," and look for words like "disease-resistant," "dependable," and "long-lasting" when you read rose descriptions.

Get started with this list of five easy-to-grow hybrid tea roses. These roses have tested well all over the country, but you should consult your neighborhood nursery for the names of other tea roses that excel in your particular climate zone.

SOME EASY-TO-GROW FORMAL ROSES

Peace (peach or pink variety)
Mr. Lincoln (red)
Queen Elizabeth (a pink grandiflora)
Tournament of Roses (a coral pink grandiflora)
Honor (white)

Note: A grandiflora is a cross between a hybrid tea and a floribunda rose. It inherits the best traits from each parent.

CHAPTER 12

CONTAINER GARDENING

Container gardening is perfect for weekend gardeners. There is practically no bending, weeding, or hoeing to worry about. You can take your gardens with you when you move or store them in the shade when you go on vacation. Container gardening allows you the freedom of putting flowers exactly where you want them, no matter what the soil is like. You don't even need a piece of ground. Hanging baskets make gardening in the sky a space-saving solution.

There is always a catch in the gardening game, and your container garden will need more passes with the watering can and require more fumbling around with fertilizers than if the same flowers were planted in the ground. There are also some other growing concerns to consider before you let your yard go to pots. A good soil mix and a good plant mix are the winning combination that will score more flowers for a lot less fuss.

POTTING SOIL FOR CONTAINER GARDENS

You will need to use a special soil mix in all your pots. Don't make the mistake of using dirt right from your garden. The soil for pots should be lightweight and free from disease. It must drain quickly, yet retain plenty of moisture. Potting soils that you buy in plastic bags at garden centers will have special additives like perlite or vermiculite, which keep the soil from packing down and suffocating your potted plants. Garden centers also sell bags of white perlite and silvery brown vermiculite to thrifty gardeners who want to mix up their own potting soil.

Cooking up your own potting soil is a quick and easy job. Here's one potting soil recipe for the gardener who's more frugal than lazy:

1. Add one part damp peat moss, one part perlite or vermiculite, and one part processed manure or compost.
2. Blend well with a hoe in a large wheelbarrow or on a tarp-covered surface. Season the mix with an all-purpose granular fertilizer, or sprinkle in a slow-release plant food like Osmacote. Use the amount recommended on the package.
3. Spoon the mixture into your pots and barrels and water well.
4. Let the "batter" stand for 24 hours or longer, then water it

again to make sure the peat moss is thoroughly saturated. Warm water does a better job of wetting peat moss than cold water. You can tell when the soil mix is ready for planting when it retains enough moisture to feel damp, but not wet.

You don't have to replace all the soil in your pots every spring. Just scrape away the dead plants and remove the top 3 inches of potting soil. Then work in a fresh layer of potting soil before adding the new plants.

If you have very large pots and plants like annuals with shallow roots, fill up the bottom half of the pots with Styrofoam pellets, or "peanuts." A layer of Styrofoam allows for good drainage, but is also lightweight and a good insulator. As long as you give your flowering plants at least 10 inches of soil to sink their roots into, you can substitute drainage material for expensive potting soil in the bottom half of any large pot.

Best Pot Spots

■ Set your pots on a bed of gravel or bricks, bordering a drive or walkway. Now you won't have to worry about stepping all over the plants if you need more room. Putting a gravel or paved surface next to a walkway or drive gives the user a more comfortable sense of space.

■ Pot up some welcoming plants near the front door, right below the doorbell.

■ Set some pots underneath trees or hang them from overhead branches. Impatiens and lobelia welcome these shady spots.

■ Hang a pot outside the kitchen window, so the blooming plant can be viewed from both inside and outside.

■ Keep containers close to you. Wherever you sit to relax and enjoy the garden is the perfect place to put a container garden.

Bigger Pots, Smaller Demands

Flowers in small pots, clay pots, and crowded pots need more water and fertilizer than container gardens planted in large tubs. It is easier to tend three large barrels of blooms than to care for six smaller pots holding the same number of flowers.

The Easiest Way to Water

A well-planned irrigation system conserves the most labor and the most water. A watering system for potted plants can be simply devised by using plastic tubing that carries water to each individual pot. Hardware stores are often a better supply source for this type of "spaghetti" tubing than nurseries and garden centers. The plastic tubing can even be pinned up the wall and then dropped over hanging baskets to discreetly water your suspended pots. Just turn on the faucet, and all your potted plants will be watered at once.

For just a few pots of flowers, invest in an easy-to-handle watering can. Park the watering can next to your pots, so that every time you see the flowers you'll be reminded that they may be thirsty.

FOOD AND THE POTTED FLOWER

All potted plants need to be fed. Plants that are growing in the ground may still bloom and grow if you don't get around to fertilizing them. This is not true for plants growing in pots!

The root systems of potted plants are trapped with a tiny source of soil, and they can't go searching the area for more nutrients. The more flowers you want, the more fertilizing you should do.

EASIEST-TO-GROW FLOWERS FOR SPRING COLOR

Primroses
Pansies
Crocus Bulbs
Dwarf Daffodil Bulbs
Snowdrop Bulbs
Short-Stemmed Tulips

BARRELS OF BLOOMS

Recycled whiskey barrels make wonderful places to grow flowers. The half barrels are inexpensive, yet big enough to grow roses and dwarf fruit trees and still provide enough space for an edging of cascading flowers. Here's how to help your barrels blossom better:

- Fill the bottom half of the barrel with Styrofoam chunks or gravel, if all you'll be growing are shallow-rooted annuals. You will need at least a 2-inch layer of drainage material, no matter what you want to grow.
- If the rustic look of the barrel doesn't appeal to you, but the price and size does, you can paint the barrels with outdoor deck paint or build a bottomless box around the tub using any type of siding.
- Filling up a whole barrel with flowers every spring can be overwhelming, so plant an evergreen shrub in the center of the whiskey barrel and then add spring-blooming bulbs and summer-blooming annuals around the edges for seasonal color. Dwarf Alberta spruce looks like a mini Christmas tree and doesn't mind being confined to a pot for years. Hino crimson azaleas and dwarf rhododendrons have compact

root systems that adjust well to life in a barrel, so long as you keep them well watered. Choose tiny bulbs that will return every spring, such as snowdrops and crocuses for the inner border of the pot. For summer color, you can add spreading annuals like lobelia and alyssum for around the outer edges. Creeping and draping annuals will help hide the dying foliage from the spring bulbs.

EASIEST-TO-GROW FLOWERS FOR SUMMER COLOR

For Sun:	**For Shade:**
Lobelia	Geraniums
Marigolds	Impatiens
Begonias	Salvia
Alyssum	Coleus
	Nasturtiums

EASIEST-TO-GROW EVERGREEN SHRUBS FOR CONTAINERS

Rhododendrons
Boxwood
Dwarf Alberta Spruce
Japanese Holly
Junipers

Index

MAR 0 7